CULTURAL

COMPETENCE FOR

GLOBAL

MANAGEMENT

Chima Imoh (Ph.D., Public Policy

and Leadership)

Heritage Publishing Company

Houston, United States of America

i

Heritage Publishing Company,
7447 Harwin Drive,
Houston, TX 77036.

Library of Congress control Number:
2012911438

Imoh, Chima

Cultural Competence for Global
Management/Chima Imoh
P.cm.-(culture, effects and problems)

ISBN-978-0985479213
  1. Cultural Competence-Business
     practices-workplaces.
  2. Global management-cultural aspects-
     organizational practices. I. Title. II.
     Series

Printed in the United States of America

PREFACE

Culture is the way of life of a group of people, which includes knowledge, beliefs, arts, morals, customs, and other capabilities and habits acquired by them as members of a particular society. The importance of cultures and nationalities lies in the knowledge that individual identities derive from them and thinking is partly conditioned by them. The culture of an individual therefore has an impact on behaviors, expectations, and tendencies. The global integration and interaction in business, governance and shared international problems involve different cultures, thereby creating high levels of cultural diversity in workplaces, in interactions, and around negotiation tables. This cultural diversity can lead to a unique set of challenges as the individuals from different cultures interact. Substantial numbers of staff members of embassies, multinational organizations, multinational companies (MNC), national and multinational armed forces, and international nonprofit and charitable organizations operate in multiple regions, each with distinct cultures and subcultures. The global environments entail that those individuals from different races and cultures; with different values, expectations and perspectives work together to achieve common goals or resolve common problems. The importance of understanding the ethical values of these different cultures is appreciable because whereas most organizations and professions have codified sets of ethical rules, cultures do not.

Cultural relationships and differences, including values, norms, moralities, and ethics do not only exist between nations, but also exist in varying magnitudes. Each culture has its own distinctive features, and ensuring success in foreign assignments requires deep understanding of the cultural differences. Most countries have embassies; multinational organizations have subsidiaries and partners in multiple regions, each with distinct cultures and subcultures, which create a unique set of cross-cultural challenges. In these foreign settings, the understanding of and approaches to administrative issues such as motivation, performance evaluation, team building and leadership also differ across cultures. Therefore, the awareness of these differences will help public officials overcome the problems posed by cultural differences.

Anyone travelling abroad is most likely to experience situations that demonstrate differences in food, dress, hygiene, altitudes, and general behavior. To a tourist or visiting business person, the experience may be exotic and enjoyable. To public servants, employees, or expatriate who are required to live and work in this new culture, however, the experience may be challenging. Persons who work or serve abroad usually face problems of adjustment to new environments. Some even lack the proper motivation for a foreign assignment, whereas some experience huge cultural shock.

Although cultural traits found in a particular country represent only the central tendencies, the importance of cultural perspectives in understanding the different attitudes toward work habits, authority, teamwork, negotiations in international settings is quite obvious. Some major cultural constraints, therefore confront these individuals and organizations as they operate overseas. These constraints arise from the unfamiliar factors and problems that are associated with the international environments and value systems. The first constraint is the cultural diversity of the international environments and the effects such have on the ways people work in and manage companies and organizations. The second constraint is the ethical issues related to dealing with different values and ethical standards. The problems posed by these cultural differences are reduced by the awareness of the differences in cultural values and beliefs, verbal and nonverbal communication patterns, and approaches to decision making and conflict resolution. Moreover, possessing a favorable disposition toward learning about other cultures helps in the establishment of rapport among interacting parties in international settings.

The improper management of the cultural diversities that naturally exist in foreign assignments and organizations can, hence, lead to miscommunication that could disrupt workplace cohesion. However, granted that the diversity inherent in multicultural organizations presents some problems, some obvious advantages also arise from them. For example, culturally diverse workplaces can enhance creativity, lead to better decision-making processes, and result in effectiveness and higher productivity. A monocultural workplace does not enjoy the benefit of diverse opinions, a multitalented worker pool, and multiple propensities for creativity. Cultural diversity also prevents one-way thinking (groupthink) by which group members are culturally pressured to agree with mainstream thinking. Sound cross-cultural competence is of immense importance to successful foreign assignment or management. It is critical, therefore, to employ, train, develop, and retain officials who not only have technical expertise but also possess cross-cultural competences, knowledge, and experiences. This book examines the cultural issues involved in working or serving abroad and makes recommendations to help private, public, international and government nonprofit organizations achieve the desired goal of improved management and productivity by their officials who serve abroad.

Chima Imoh, Ph.D.

ABOUT THE AUTHOR

Chima Imoh has a degree in Geodetic Engineering and a master's degree in international management. He has a doctorate degree in Public policy and Administration, specializing in public management and leadership. Dr Imoh is a member of the National Honor Society for Public Affairs and Administration, United States of America. The author has lectured and worked in public institutions in the United States and in Africa. Dr Chima Imoh is a co-author of the book, *Competence for Public Administration,* edited by Dr Susan T. Gooden and Dr Kris Major.

CONTENTS

Chapter 1: The Cultural Dynamics of Societies...1

Chapter 2: World-wide National Cultural Orientation..................15

Chapter 3: Impacts of Culture on Communication.....................28

Chapter 4: Impacts of Culture on Business Relationships...............33

Chapter 5: Impacts of Culture on Workplace Attitudes................37

Chapter 6: Impacts of National Culture on Organizational Cultures and Structures......................39

Chapter 7: Impacts of Culture on Organizational Behavior and Management.......................44

Chapter 8: Impacts of Culture on Work Teams........................51

Chapter 9: Impacts of Culture on Organizational leadership...........62

Chapter 10: Impacts of Culture on International Negotiations..........69

Chapter 11: Impacts of Culture on International Alliances and Joint Ventures.......................................75

Chapter 12: Rules of Thumbs for Managing Across Cultures........83

Chapter 13: Organizational Strategies for Developing Global Management Skill...................92

Chapter 14: Cultural Competence for Global Managers................99

Chapter 15: Ethical Issues in Global Management..............105

Chapter 16: Summaries of Business and Work Attitudes of National Clusters........................109

Chapter 17: Snapshots of Work and Organizational Attitudes in Some Nations…………..………...118

Appendix………..…………..…......129

Endnotes…………..………...…131

Chapter 1
The Cultural Dynamics of Societies

Cultural orientation forms values, creates attitudes and influences behavior of the individual. The existence and importance of the relationships between cultural systems and organizational practices are, therefore, worth appreciating. With the associated cultures, more than 3,000 different languages are spoken worldwide[1]. These cultural systems can permeate all levels of organizations, and those engaged in cross-national relationships and interactions need to be concerned with these cross-cultural issues[2]. In studying the cultural orientation of societies, the Dutch scholar Geert Hofstede analyzed cultural behavior of the individual on the basis of power distance, individualism, collectivism, masculinity, femininity, and uncertainty avoidance[3]. In simple terms, these respectively mean the analysis of how people accept social inequality (power distance), the bonds between the individual and his or her societal groups (individualism versus collectivism), the extent to which the individual embraces the competitive masculine orientation or the nurturing feminine traits (masculinity versus femininity), and the extent to which people strive to control their situations (uncertainty avoidance). Hofstede explained the cultural tendency of the various nationalities through these dimensions.

Hofstede's Cultural Dimensions

Individualism versus Collectivism

Individualism reflects situation where the relations between an individual and other individuals in the society are very loose[4]. In the individualistic cultural societies such as the United States, Canada; and the Anglo, Germanic, and Nordic Europe, individuals look after their own self-interests or the interest of small groups to which they are ties such as the immediate family[5]. These individualistic cultures value autonomy, competition, self-determination, and pursuit of self-interest[6]. The very individualistic countries are the United States, Great Britain[7]. Employees in individualistic societies crave the feelings of personal accomplishment and individual recognition for a job well done and for efforts that exceed those of others[8]. These needs for personal recognition foster an appreciation for competition[9].

Individualism implies such societies as the United States that have high degrees of freedom where individuals are expected to look after their own interests. In individualistic cultures, the individual is assumed to be self-motivated and self-actualized, with self-interest defining relationships. The need of the individual is valued over collective, or group, needs. This dimension of culture emphasizes the protection of self-image and freedom from imposition. This dimension reflects the degree to which people are encouraged to integrate into groups within the society[10].

In the individualistic societies, individuals are seen

as autonomous entities who find meaning and opportunities in their own uniqueness by following their own ideas. Individuals value curiosity, creativity, and open-mindedness, while pursuing positive experiences that make them feel good. In these societies, one's identity is defined by one's own life history and choices and individuals are linked by rules that are assumed to apply equally to all[11].

Conversely, a collectivist cultural type (low individualism) reflects a situation where strong social ties exist among societal members, with each member primarily concerned with the prevailing interest of the in-group[12]. In collectivist societies of Asia, Africa, and Latin America, members of a group tend to similar beliefs, working a feeling of harmonious interdependence[13].

The collectivist cultures emphasize social duty and the impacts of one's actions on others[14]. People mostly derive their identities from one's connection to in-groups such as family, clan, or employer [15]. These concerns for entities larger than oneself foster an appreciation for cooperation, harmony, conformity, and loyalty[16]. The very collectivist countries are Colombia, Pakistan, and Taiwan[17]. The United States, United Kingdom, Netherlands, France and the Nordic countries are highly individualistic; whereas the Latin American and Asian countries tend to be highly collectivist[18].

On the other hand, collectivism (otherwise called low individualism) applies to societies in which individuals expect others in the groups to which they belong to protect their interests, and in exchange the individuals incline toward group loyalty. This collectivism emphasizes in-group solidarity, loyalty, and interdependence among individuals. In these societies, individuals are viewed as part of the group, and meaning in life comes from social relationships, group identification, and participation in shared ways of life and goals. One's identity is defined by one's position in a family or in a hierarchically ordered societal group[19]. These societies value social ordering, respect for tradition, and collective security. In addition, relationships within a collectivist cultural type are strong and intimate[20].

The concept of individualism reflects the value of loosely knit social relationships in which individuals are expected to take care of themselves, whereas collectivism reflects a preference for closer social networks in which individuals tend to look after one another[21]. The concept of collectivism also emphasizes the interdependence between the self and one's group or community[22]. Hence, collectivists place high value on collective goals, guided by group norms and authority figures[23].

Masculinity versus Femininity

Masculine cultures place high value on assertiveness, independence, task orientation, and self-achievement, whereas feminine cultures value cooperation, relationship, empathy for the less fortunate, moderation, and preference for relationships. Masculinity is the male-oriented inclination to assertiveness and competition. Such societies as the United States, high in masculinity, emphasize assertiveness, acquisition of money, and material goods, while deemphasizing concern for others.

The most masculine countries are, however, Japan and the Latin American countries. These masculinity culture countries always strive for a performance society. On the other hand, femininity (also called low masculinity) emphasizes relationships, concern for others, and quality of life.

The most feminine societies are the Nordic countries of Sweden, Denmark, Norway, Netherlands and Finland[24]. These femininity culture countries strive for a welfare society by emphasizing cooperation, moderation, and empathy for the less fortunate. The Latin European countries, France, Spain, Portugal, Chile, and South Korea have moderate femininity.

The most masculine country is Japan, followed by Germany, Switzer and Austria[25] and the Latin American countries. The countries moderate in masculinity are United States, Great Britain and the other Anglo countries; Asia countries, African countries, Italy, and India[26].

Power Distance

Power distance refers to the manner a societies addresses physical, material and intellectual inequalities within its structure and politic. Some cultural types allow inequalities to grow over time until there is great separation of power and wealth, whereas others attempt to minimize the inequalities by redistributing power and wealth[27]. The cultural types that allow inequalities to grow are termed high power distance, while those that minimize inequalities are termed low power distance[28].

Power distance implies the degree to which status,

wealth, or power differences are acceptable to a society. In low power distance societies, individuals strive for power equalization and justice. Power distance reflects the level at which people are comfortable with inequalities in the wielding of power among institutions and people.[29]

Power distance is also a construct that refers to the degree to which relationships between individuals in a society are hierarchical[30]. This dimension indicates how a society stratifies its individuals and groups with respect to power, authority, prestige, status, wealth and other material possessions[31].

The low power distance Anglo-American, Nordic, and Germanic cultures place more emphasis on competence than on seniority. These cultures minimize inequalities, favor less autocratic leaders, and favor less centralization of authority.

High power distance societies are usually status-conscious, respecting age and seniority, bestowing outward importance on protocol, formality, and hierarchy. Very high power distance societies, such as China, France, India, Turkey, Thailand, Saudi Arabia, Nigeria, Venezuela, Malaysia, Mexico, and the Philippines, accept and support large imbalances in power, status, and wealth; much respect is shown for those in authority; and titles, ranks, and status are revered. These cultures have greater acceptance for inequalities and authoritarian leadership. The other high power distance cultures are the other Latin American, South Asia, and Arabic cultures. The low power distance countries are the Anglo-American, Nordic, and Germanic cultures that include Austria, Israel, and Demark. France,

Belgium, Japan, Korea, Spain and Italy are fairly high.

Uncertainty Avoidance

Uncertainty avoidance refers to the degree of tolerance or acceptance a society has for surprises, ambiguity, risk, or chance factors[32]. This dimension also refers to the extent to which people seek orderliness, consistency, structure and laws[33]. This dimension also refers to the degree to which individuals in the society feel uncomfortable in risky, uncertain, or unpredictable situations and the degree to which the society favors conformity or is tolerant of deviant ideas.

In such high uncertainty avoidance societies as Iran, China, Mexico, and Italy, people feel threatened by uncertainty and show little tolerance for deviation. The high uncertainty avoidance societies try to create security and avoid risks by using such instruments as rules and laws, expertise and formal institutions, or religion. In low uncertainty avoidance societies as the United States, the Nordic countries, and the United Kingdom, people are reasonably tolerant of different behaviors and opinions, do not feel threatened by such differences, and are also willing to accept personal risk.

The strong uncertainty avoidance cultural types attempt to formulate ways of controlling future events, thereby reducing the level of uncertainty and risks[34]. The weak uncertainty avoidance cultural types accept higher levels of risk and therefore do not attempt to control uncertainty, but rather socialize members of the society to accept it[35].

From a study of 50 countries, Hofstede[36] concluded as

follows:

(i) Some countries, namely; France, Belgium, Italy, Spain, Czech, Slovakia, Greece, Turkey, Japan, Korea; and the Latin American countries show both high power distance and high uncertainty avoidance.

(ii) Most Asian and African countries, namely; Philippines, Malaysia, Indonesia, Singapore, Hong Kong, India, Nigeria, Ghana, Kenya, Ethiopia and Zambia have high power distance and medium to weak uncertainty avoidance.

(iii) The Germanic-speaking countries-Austria, Switzerland, Germany, Israel, and Finland, combine small power distance and medium to strong uncertainty avoidance.

(iv) Denmark, Sweden, Great Britain and Ireland have small power distance and weak uncertainty avoidance.

(v) Netherlands, United States, Norway, Canada, Australia, and New Zealand have low to moderate power distance and uncertainty avoidance.

There is, however, a global relationship between power distance and collectivism[37]. The collectivist countries always show high power distance. It is noteworthy that individualistic countries do not always show low power distance as exemplified by the Latin European countries -France, Belgium, Italy and Spain- that show fairly high power distances and high individualism[38]. With the exception of these countries, all other wealthy western countries have a combination of small power distance and individualism[39]. Conversely, all poor countries are collectivist and also have large power distances[40].

Short-term versus Long-term Orientation

The influence of the Confucian philosophy manifests on this dimension that Geert Hofstede later developed. The long-term orientation indicates a focus on the future. The long-term orientation anchors actions and thoughts more to the future than in the past and present. The people of east Asia, namely; China, Philippines, Hong Kong, Malaysia, Singapore, Taiwan, Indonesia, South Vietnam, and Thailand are characterized by long-term orientation.

These cultures are more likely to emphasize education, training, thriftiness and delay of immediate gratification. They are also likely to prefer long-term rather than short-term relationships. Moreover, countries with this cultural orientation usually regard family harmony and relationships as the foundation on which societies are organized, and, therefore stress family and kinship relations when doing business[41]. The short-term orientation places more emphasis on the past and present. Such short-term oriented cultures show deep respect for tradition and for the fulfillment of social obligations.

Hofstede's study are relevant to organizational behavior, structure, and leadership; negotiation attitudes, work ethics, business relations; and alliances and joint venture management in a country. Geert Hofstede had illustrated the relevance of these dimensions with the following questions[42].

(i)   Power distance: How much do people in a given society expect and condone inequality is social institutions, family, workplace, organizations and government?

(ii)   Individualism-collectivism: How tight or loose is the bond between individuals and societal groups in daily lives and workplaces?

(iii) Masculinity-femininity: To what extent do people embrace such competitive masculine tendencies as success, assertiveness and performance or such nurturing feminine behaviors as solidarity, personal relationship, and service, quality of life in daily lives, business dealings, and workplaces?

(iv)   Uncertainty avoidance: To what extent do people prefer structured situations as against unstructured situations in the daily lives, business transactions and workplaces?

(v)   Short-long term orientation: To what extent do people prefer long term as against short term situations in planning, expecting returns or gratifications?

Trompenaar's Cultural Dimensions

In their 1998 book, *The Seven Cultures of Capitalism,* Fons Trompenaars and Charles Hampden-Turner had found seven cultural values for explaining differences in such organizational behaviors as decision making, hiring, rewarding employees and making rules[43]. These dimensions also focused on how societies develop approaches toward managing problems and difficult situations. In this study, they used the term communitarianism rather than collectivism. To avoid any confusion, however, the term collectivism will, hereafter, be used.

Universalism versus particularism

Universalism and particularism deal with the standards by which relationships are measured. The Universalist societies tend to portray that general rules and obligations are strong sources of moral behaviors. Individuals in these societies are inclined to apply the rules and regulations, even when friends and relatives are involved, striving for equity and fairness to all. They always assume that their standards are that right standards and, therefore, strive to change the attitudes and beliefs of others to match theirs. In particularistic societies on the other hand, circumstances are more important than the rules. The bonds of family and friendly relationships are usually stronger than rules and regulations.

Individualism versus Communitarianism

Individualism and communitarianism dimensions in Trompenaar's and Hampden-Turner's studies analyze the interest of the individual as against the interest of the group to which the individual belongs. This dimension is similar to the individualism- collectivism dimension of Geert Hofstede. In individualistic societies, individuals are expected to make their own decisions, only taking care of themselves and their immediate family. These societies give priority to freedom and choice. The general in such societies is that the quality of life enjoyed by individuals result from their efforts. In communitarian societies, individuals are integrated into groups that are expected to provide help and protection in exchange for loyalty. In such societies, the group comes before the individual; hence, people are expected to be oriented toward common goals and objectives.

Specific versus Diffuse

These dimensions deal with how people analyze situations. People from specifically oriented culture begin by analyzing the elements of a situation separately, and then putting back the parts again to form the whole. People from diffusely oriented cultures view each element as complete, but related to each other. This dimension also measures the extent to which individuals get involved with others' lives. In specific-oriented cultures, leaders and managers often separate work relationship from other dealings. In diffused cultures, work relationships usually permeate private lives.

Neutral versus Affective

These deal with the interplay of reason and emotion in human relationships. In cultures that are emotionally neutral, individuals strive to control their emotions and are, therefore, reluctant to show their feelings. In these cultures, reason tends to dominate emotions when interacting with others. On the contrast, cultures that are high on affectivity, people freely express their feelings, and it is quite acceptable to show one's feeling spontaneously.

Achievement versus ascription

The achievement and ascription dimensions deal with whether personal status is assigned or acquired through performance. The achievement societies accord people respect based on their performance. The ascription societies, on the other hand, accord status and respect based on such issues as pedigree, age, class, gender, education etcetera.

Internal versus external

These are dimensions concerning the meaning individuals attach to the external environment. Cultures that have internalized perspective belief one can dominate nature. Cultures that are externally controlled view of nature, in contrast, belief that man is controlled by nature. This culture tends to attribute events and situations to destiny. Individuals in this culture orient their actions towards others and their environments rather than themselves. More than the western cultures, the East Asian and Arabic cultures are externally centered, alluding to fate as an explanation for personal outcomes.

Time orientation

This is the dimension dealing with the relative importance with which the culture structures time; whether it does so sequentially or synchronously.

Cultures with sequential perception of time tend to perceive time as a series of passing events; doing one thing at a time, and planning and keeping to plans. Commitments to time and schedule are taken seriously. On the other hand, cultures that structure time synchronically perceive the past, present and future as interrelated events; and thereby doing multiple things at the same time. Commitments to time and schedule are desirable, but are not absolute, and therefore, can be easily be subjected to changes.

Chapter 2
World-wide National Cultural Orientation

The worldwide cultural orientation of clusters of nations can be summarized and tabulated as shown in the tables below. It is essential to point out that cultures change gradually over time, and that the sub-cultures vary in some ways from the national culture. Moreover, people who have worked or lived outside their own countries may pick up some behaviors or attitudes from other cultures.

From the effects of these cultural dimensions on national and organizational system, Simcha Ronen and Oded Shenkar [1] developed clusters of countries with similar work values, geographic location, language and religion. These are:

Anglo Countries (United States, Canada, Australia, the United Kingdom, New Zealand, and Ireland).

These countries are high in individualism, high in masculinity, low to moderate in power distance, and low to medium in uncertainty avoidance. The high individualism of these cultures means that people ideally strive for personal achievements while accepting personal responsibility for successes as well as failures. In such low power distance societies as the United States, subordinates and superiors perceive and treat each other as colleagues who have equal rights, with the subordinates expecting to have inputs in the decisions or actions affecting them[2].

With their low to medium uncertainty avoidance orientation, these societies socialize their members into accepting uncertainty and not becoming upset by it. Members of these societies are relatively more tolerant of behaviors and opinions that differ from theirs because they not feel threatened by them. The people of these societies have the tendency to feel secured. The leadership styles in such societies are often participatory.

These countries also have universalistic rule-based cultures. In these countries the focus is more on rules than relationships, and legal contracts are readily drawn up. A trustworthy individual honors a contract because "a deal is a deal". These cultures also have strong belief in standard operating procedures. When organizations from this cluster operate abroad, rather appreciating the cultural differences and embracing the need for cultural sensitivity training, they prefer to identify and empower the 5% of the local employees that fit into their value system.

The individuals from countries in this cluster will likely be affective in their emotions, and will express their feeling in a first business contact, not feel awkward at public display of emotions, and may not displeasure with physical contact, gesturing and strong facial expressions. In these specific cultures, private and business lives are separated, and the relationship between individual depends on the common ground at that moment. The use of title varies with the circumstance and reflects the situation. Official titles are separated from private lives. These societies value specialization, and respect the opinion of experts. These are also achievement societies that place emphasis on what one has accomplished rather than the personality of the individual.

The Germanic countries (Switzerland, Germany, and Austria).

These countries are moderate in individualism, moderate in masculinity, moderate in uncertainty avoidance, and low in power distance. The high individualism of these cultures means that people ideally strive for personal achievements while accepting personal responsibility for successes as well as failures. In these low power distance societies, subordinates and superiors perceive and treat each other as colleagues who have equal rights.

With their low to medium uncertainty avoidance orientation, these societies socialize their members into accepting uncertainty and not becoming upset by it. Members of these societies are relatively more tolerant of behaviors and opinions that differ from theirs because they not feel threatened by them. The people of these societies have the tendency to feel secured.

These countries also have universalistic rule-based cultures. In these countries the focus is more on rules than relationships, and legal contracts are readily drawn up. A trustworthy individual honors a contract because "a deal is a deal". The individuals from countries in this cluster will likely be neutral in their emotions, and will hardly express their feeling in a first business contact, feel awkward at public display of emotions, and could displeasure with physical contact outside 'private' circles.

The Nordic countries (Sweden, Denmark, Norway, Finland, and The Netherlands).

The countries are moderate in individualism and uncertainty avoidance, and are low in masculinity and power distance. With their low to medium uncertainty avoidance orientation, these societies socialize their members into accepting uncertainty and not becoming upset by it. Members of these societies are relatively more tolerant of behaviors and opinions that differ from theirs because they not feel threatened by them. The people of these societies have the tendency to feel secured.

In these low power distance societies, subordinates and superiors perceive and treat each other as colleagues who have equal rights. These countries also have universalistic rule-based cultures. In these countries the focus is more on rules than relationships, and legal contracts are readily drawn up. A trustworthy individual honors a contract because "a deal is a deal". The individuals from countries in this cluster will likely be neutral in their emotions, and will hardly express their feeling in a first business contact, feel awkward at public display of emotions, and could displeasure with physical contact outside 'private' circles.

The Near Eastern countries (Greece, Iran, Yugoslavia, and Turkey)

These countries are low in individualism (collectivism), moderate in masculinity, and high in power distance and high uncertainty avoidance. In these collectivist societies, people tend to achieve jointly as well as assume joint responsibility. In negotiations people from these cultures, decisions usually taken after prior discussions, and prior consent of colleagues or bosses. These cultures are always reluctant to follow the pay-for-performance system of the Anglo-Saxon societies.

These high uncertainty avoidance societies try to socialize the people into trying to beat the future because the future is unpredictable. In these societies, there is usually higher anxiety, leading to nervousness. These societies try to create security and avoid risk by using such instruments as laws or religion to protect the society from the unpredictability of human behaviors. The proliferation of laws implies intolerance for deviant behaviors and opinions. Alternatively, they use religion use to make the uncertainty tolerable because religions contain teachings that they believe are beyond uncertainty. Usually, there is always one religion that claim absolute truth; thereby showing little tolerance for other religions.

By contrast, in such high power distance societies as the Arab, Asian, and African countries, superiors expect to lead and make decisions. The leadership styles in such societies are predominantly autocratic or paternalistic.

The Arabic Countries (Saudi Arabia, United Arab Emirates, Bahrain, Kuwait, Oman, Abu-Dhabi, Bahrain, Egypt, Iraq, Kuwait, Lebanon, Libya, Oman, Saudi Arabia, United Arab Emirates).

These countries are low in individualism (collectivism), moderate in masculinity and high in uncertainty avoidance, and high in power distance. The cultural orientations of these societies have been influence largely by the Moslem religion. In these collectivist societies, people tend to achieve jointly as well as assume joint responsibility. These societies have high power distance that indicates high level of inequality of power and wealth; high uncertainty avoidance, that indicates low level of tolerance for uncertainty; and moderate masculinity that indicates that it is religion, rather than culture that limits the rights of women in these societies. These societies are also collectivist, indicating long-term commitment to groups and common interests.

These high uncertainty avoidance societies try to socialize the people into trying to beat the future because the future is unpredictable. In these societies, there is usually higher anxiety, leading to nervousness. These societies try to create security and avoid risk by using such instruments as laws or religion to protect the society from the unpredictability of human behaviors. The proliferation of laws implies intolerance for deviant behaviors and opinions. Alternatively, they use religion use to make the uncertainty tolerable because religions contain teachings that they believe are beyond uncertainty. Usually, there is always one religion that claim absolute truth; thereby showing little tolerance for other religions.

These Arab countries, predominantly sharing the characteristics of large power distance and high uncertainty avoidance are, therefore, more likely to condone hierarchical systems that do not encourage significant upward mobility of its citizens. The societies use laws, rules, regulations, and controls that do not often protect the rights and interest of the citizens, but rather to reduce the amount of uncertainty in the societies. The societies also condone the inequalities of wealth and power within them. These dimensions of high power distance and high uncertainty avoidance also create situations where the leaders virtually wield ultimate power and authority, developing and using laws and rules to maintain their leadership and control.

The Far Eastern countries (the Philippines, Hong Kong, Malaysia, Singapore, Taiwan, Indonesia, South Vietnam, and Thailand).

These counties are low in individualism (collectivism), moderate in masculinity and low to medium in uncertainty avoidance, and high in power distance. This cluster is largely under the influence of the Confucian philosophy. In these collectivist societies, people tend to achieve jointly as well as assume joint responsibility. These societies have high power distance that indicates high level of inequality of power and wealth. These are particularistic cultures where everything depends on the circumstances and relationships. These cultures favor on the job training that is more likely to capture the realities, over formal training.

With their low to medium uncertainty avoidance orientation, these societies socialize their members into accepting uncertainty and not becoming upset by it. Members of these societies are relatively more tolerant of behaviors and opinions that differ from theirs because they not feel threatened by them. The people of these societies have the tendency to feel secured.

The individuals from countries in this cluster will likely be neutral in their emotions, and will hardly express their feeling in a first business contact, feel awkward at public display of emotions, and could displeasure with physical contact outside 'private' circles.

Latin American countries (Argentina, Venezuela, Chile, Mexico, Peru, and Colombia)

The countries are low in individualism and high in masculinity, high in power distance, and high in uncertainty avoidance. In these collectivist societies, people tend to achieve jointly as well as assume joint responsibility. These societies have high power distance that indicates high level of inequality of power and wealth; high uncertainty avoidance, which indicates low level of tolerance for uncertainty.

These high uncertainty avoidance societies try to socialize the people into trying to beat the future because the future is unpredictable. In these societies, there is usually higher anxiety, leading to nervousness. These societies try to create security and avoid risk by using such instruments as laws or religion to protect the society from the unpredictability of human behaviors. The proliferation of laws implies intolerance for deviant behaviors and opinions. Alternatively, they use religion use to make the uncertainty tolerable because religions contain teachings that they believe are beyond uncertainty. Usually, there is always one religion that claim absolute truth; thereby showing little tolerance for other religions.

Latin European countries (France, Belgium, Italy, Spain, and Portugal)

They are moderate in individualism and high in masculinity, high in power distance, and high in uncertainty avoidance. These societies have high power distance that indicates high level of inequality of power and wealth; high uncertainty avoidance, which indicates low level of tolerance for uncertainty.

These high uncertainty avoidance societies try to socialize the people into trying to beat the future because the future is unpredictable. In these societies, there is usually higher anxiety, leading to nervousness. These societies try to create security and avoid risk by using such instruments as expert opinions or religion to protect the society from the unpredictability of human behaviors. They rely on expert opinions because such is assumed to be beyond uncertainty. These societies also use religion use to make the uncertainty tolerable because religions contain teachings that they believe are beyond uncertainty. Usually, there is always one religion that claim absolute truth; thereby showing little tolerance for other religions.

The combination of high power distance and high

uncertainty avoidance in these societies, in general, leads to relatively high centralization of decision making process than other European countries with moderate levels of both cultural dimensions. Moreover, organizations in these societies have hierarchical structures.

In these particularistic societies, the focus is more on relationship than rules; and legal contracts are readily modified. The trustworthy person is one who appreciates and honors changing circumstances, knowing that relationships evolve. Individuals from these countries do not hesitate to show their emotions, ether verbally or nonverbally. In these diffused societies also, one's official life also permeates the private and every other area of life. Interpersonal relationships are all encompassing involving official, private and every other facet of life. For instance, one's official titles are also used in private settings.

Sub-Saharan Africa countries (Nigeria, Ghana, Kenya, Ethiopia, Zambia and Sierra Leone).

These countries are representative of other others in the Sub-Saharan Africa. The sub-Saharan Africa countries are mostly inhabited by the Negroid (black) races of Africa. The countries of this region are the 49 nations that share common history of the slave trade, colonization and underdevelopment. They are low in individualism, high in power distance, and moderate in uncertainty avoidance and moderate masculinity. These societies have high power distance that indicates high level of inequality of power and wealth.

The Independents (Brazil, China, India, Israel, Pakistan, South Africa, and Japan).

These countries did not fit into any classification of the clusters. The economic development and technological advancement of these countries have created an override on the cultural tendencies of their geographical groupings[3]. This, however, excludes China whose uniqueness on rest communism, its political and economic system.

Brazil has a mixture of races, religions and cultures[4]. Research studies have variously placed Brazil in the Latin European cluster and as an independent[5]. Brazil is on moderate levels of masculinity and individualism, strong uncertainty avoidance, and high power distance. The Brazilian institutions operate both through personal relationships and on rules. This society lies between the Anglo culture of egalitarianism and hierarchical culture of the high power distance societies.

Although Chinese culture, as the culture of the other far (east) Asian countries, is built largely on the Confucian philosophy, its political and economic system differentiates the country from the cluster. In contrast therefore, China is low on individualism, high on power distance, but high in uncertainty avoidance and in masculinity.

India has variously been placed in the Anglo cluster, the Latin American cluster, and the Far East cluster[6]. India is high in power distance, weak in uncertainty avoidance, low in individualism (collectivism) and high in masculinity. The collectivism of the India society creates an emphasis on group orientation; whereas the high dominance of power distance and masculinity creates high level of bureaucracy and acceptance of caste systems.

Studies have variously placed Israel in the Anglo cluster and the Germanic cluster[7]. The Israeli culture shares low power distance with such countries as Denmark and Austria, medium in individualism and masculinity, and strong uncertainty avoidance. This high uncertainty avoidance society tries to socialize the people into trying to beat the future, create security and avoid risk by using such instruments as expert opinions, laws and religion to protect the society from the unpredictability of human behaviors. They rely on expert opinions because such is assumed to be beyond uncertainty. The proliferation of laws implies intolerance for deviant behaviors and opinions. Alternatively, they use religion use to make the uncertainty tolerable because religions contain teachings that they believe are beyond uncertainty. Usually, there is always one religion that claim absolute truth; thereby showing little tolerance for other religions.

Iran had been earlier been placed by outside its geographical zone into the near East cluster by Hofstede[8]. Unlike its immediate neighbors, Iran has moderation power distance, masculinity, individualism and uncertainty avoidance orientation.

Japan had earlier been placed in the Far East cluster by Redding[9]. The country is the most masculine country, has strong uncertainty avoidance, moderate power distance, moderate in individualism[10].

Pakistan had earlier been placed with India into the

Far East cluster[11]. Just like India; religion has had enormous effects on the culture of Pakistan. Pakistan has low individualism, high power distance, strong uncertainty avoidance, and medium masculinity.

For reasons of history, relatively longer years of British colonization and mixed racial composition, South Africa differs in cultural dimensions from the other African countries. South Africa demonstrates a profile of moderate power distance, moderate uncertainty avoidance, high individualism and high masculinity.

Chapter 3
Impacts of Culture on Communication

Communication is probably one of the most relevant tools for managing a multicultural organization. Every management function involves some form of direct or indirect transmission of messages[1]. The creation of effective communication sustains organizations[2]. However, cultural diversity usually presents unique challenges when people from diverse cultural backgrounds attempt to communicate effectively[3]. This diversity comes with the risks of misunderstanding that may hamper the collaboration between the concerned individuals and may adversely affect the outcomes of operations[4]. Language infiltrates so intensely, the social experience within a culture that neither language nor culture can be understood without knowledge of both[5].

The cultural orientation of the individual also impacts on the style of transmitting messages. In communication, cultures can be categorized as high-context, in which primary meaning is derived from non-verbal clues, and low-context, in which primary meaning is derived from written or spoken words. People from high context cultures rely heavily on nonverbal clues for meanings when communicating with others[6]. The non-verbal clues such as official position, status, title or family names, therefore, convey more power messages than spoken words[7]. The high-context cultures as the Chinese, Koreans, Japanese, Arabs, Greeks, Spanish, Latin American, Africans and Italian are equally collectivist and similarly, (i) they establish social trust first before business, (ii) value personal relationships and goodwill, (iii) agreement is by general trust, (iv) negotiations are slow and ritualistic (Kreitner and Kinicki, 2004). In such high-context cultures as Japan, Nigeria your business card says it all- your employer, your official position, your titles, academic attainment and even honors.

The low-context cultures are mostly the individualistic countries as the English, North American, Scandinavians, Swiss, and Germans; and similarly they, (i) get down to business first before socializing, (ii) value expertise and performance, agreements are drawn by specific legalistic contract, and (iv) negotiations are as timely as possible[8].

For instance, low-context cultures tend to communicate by as explicit and detailed means as possible. Hence, communication in the low-context Western culture is typically direct and explicit[9]. This contrasts with high-context cultures, in which the true meanings of communicative actions are usually hidden in the manner in which the message is conveyed or in some other nonverbal clues. For these high-context cultures, communications are implicit and indirect. For example, Chinese is a high-context culture that leaves a considerable part of a message unsaid, leaving the interpretation of the missing information to the other party[10]. The Chinese therefore tend to avoid stating their intentions directly and expressing their emotions overtly[11.] Because of these differences, communication between people of different contextual backgrounds may suffer from misunderstandings because it either conveys too much or too little information[12].

The cultural orientation of the individual imparts on the style of communication. Hence, cultural diversity usually presents unique challenges to the issue of how people from diverse cultural backgrounds attempt to effectively communicate on daily basis[13]. Among the Arabs, Africans, and Asians, a great deal of indirect and nonverbal communication takes place. In contrast, in the United States the style of communication is concise, direct, and explicit.

The global business environment has essentially become multinational and multicultural, leading to a growing need for effective communication. Multicultural communication has, therefore, become the bedrock of international business. International business is the life blood of many of today's enterprises and brings executives into face-to-face contact with other executives of totally different cultural backgrounds[14]. It has become evident that persons of dissimilar cultures are having more difficulties communicating effectively than they are with those from the same culture[15]. This internationalization of the organizational workforce therefore requires that global managers become conscious of the communications procedures and conventions of foreign cultures, especially those relevant to their duties and functions. The need to make communication more effective by involving cultural awareness, sensitivity, and understanding has increased[16].

Effective communication in international settings depends; however, on the ability to construct common-sense communication[17]. Each culture has its own distinct manner of exchanging messages (verbal and nonverbal). Therefore, ensuring the success of a foreign posting would require a deep understanding of cultural differences. By understanding the models of different cultures, global managers can create strategies for dealing and negotiating with different cultures[18]. Otherwise, if the operations of multicultural teams become hindered by poor communications, the long-term goals of the organization or department could be jeopardized.

The differences in languages would likely create some communication problems. Since a mutual understanding of a particular language does not exist organization may resort to the use of translators. Translations would be necessary here, even though they bring about their own peculiar problems. Live translations, translations of written documents and advertisements, and computer email translations are helpful but plagued by accuracy problems[19]. It is necessary that the visiting business teams provide the translators. In this way, it would be assumed that complete allegiance would be to them.

Despite these differences, the strategies for improving cross cultural communication include the development of communication competence through training. The essence of communication competence training would be to sensitize the workers as to the differences is cultural orientation and culture-dependent differences in attitudes, values and work styles and communication styles. Communication competence as the ability to apply language skills to situations; and   concluded that it means making good use of communication to effectively attain goals[20]. When communicating in a multi-cultural environment, therefore, managers should ensure that both the spoken and written languages are clear and concise. Global managers are, therefore, advised to communicate clearly and make sure all verbal as well as non-verbal communications are clear, reliable and consistent[21].

Chapter 4
Impacts of Culture on Business Relationships

There is a major relationship between the cultural orientation of any human being and his/her working and business practices. Individuals from individualistic cultures are usually competitive and tend to accept personal responsibility. Personal relationships and interactions usually have positive impacts on cross-cultural interactions with individuals from collectivist cultures. Such collectivist societies as Saudis Arabia attach a great deal of importance to status. Such collectivist societies usually conduct business only after trust has been well established.

People from such universalistic countries as always believe that practices can be applied everywhere without modification. Individuals in such countries as United States, Canada, Australia, United Kingdom, Germany, and Denmark therefore tend to focus on formal rules and expect their business associates to do the same. These cultures are usually value directness and task orientation. In business dealings, therefore, these cultures place less emphasis on personal relationship and focus more on the tasks[1].

On the other hand, people from such particularistic

cultures believe that circumstances should dictate how practices should be applied. Individuals in such countries as France, Italy, Spain, Portugal, Philippines, Malaysia, Indonesia, and Thailand, therefore, tend to focus on relationships; working things out to suit their business partners. In these particularistic societies, bonds of friendship and relationship are usually stronger than rules; and individuals are more likely to exhibit a higher degree of nepotism or favoritism in such matters as employment, contract awards, and school admissions etcetera. In societies with particularistic cultures, relationships also play visible roles in all aspects of life; and most official and businesses are transacted on that basis. Hence, employment, organizational ascendancy, and organizational transactions are usually done on basis of personal relationship. In these societies, even official interactions are friendship-based society and more often; official assistances are rendered on the basis of personal relationship. Business opportunities revolve around the government and its agencies; and are most times, dispensed are developed through personal relationships. This seems to be a sharp contrast to what obtains in cultures with high universalism (like the U.S.), where the focus is on rules[2]. The indication here is that the global manager should expect a certain level of nepotism and favoritism especially in employment. The guideline is to endeavor to balance the necessity of building and keeping those personal relationships, while at the same maintaining the required professional standards.

In specifically oriented societies, the official and private lives are separated. This is unlike the diffusely oriented societies where relationships are in multiple spheres that involve official and private lives. In such societies, it is usual for the manager to be actively involved the private affairs of subordinates as wedding, birthday celebrations and bereavements.

In neutral emotion cultures, individuals strive to hold their emotions in check. Reasoning, rather than emotions, dominates one's interactions with business partners. Individuals from neutral culture countries as Germany, Switzerland, Netherlands, Malaysia, Indonesia, Taiwan, Hong Kong, and Thailand try not to show their feelings, whereas people from emotional culture countries as Latin America and Africa express their emotions openly and naturally: smiling, talking loud, greeting with enthusiasm, and showing both happiness and unhappiness.

In achievement societies, respect is accorded based on how well the person has performed or what the person has accomplished. Importance is, therefore placed on job, work performance, skills, and education. In the ascription societies, status and respect are accorded based on who or what the person is; and importance is placed as age, gender, family, ethnic group.

In countries that observe time from the sequential perspectives, individuals do one thing at a time, keep appointments strictly, and follow plans to the letter. Societies that observe time from the synchronous perspective do more than one thing at a time, and appointments are approximate. In such societies in which people are inner-directed, they believe the can control what happens to them, and are, therefore, architects of their own fortune or misfortunes. These are individuals in societies that are built on the protestant ethics of hard work and personal responsibility. The outer-directed people believe in allowing things take their natural course, and that they are less to control what happens to them, believing in that whatever happens to them have been destined to happen. If, therefore, a business negotiation goes bad or a contract breached, it must be due to predestination.

It is, for instance, not so beneficial to send junior managers to business meetings with senior Saudi executives who would surely feel slighted by such. Another perspective to note is that "disagreeing with an Arab in the presence of others is an impoliteness that may be difficult to remedy[3]. The Arabs attach a great deal of importance to status and rank and that it is also important never to criticize or berate anyone in public[4].

With their long-term orientation and collectivism, the East Asian cultures are more likely to emphasize education, training, thriftiness and delay of immediate gratification. They are also likely to prefer long-term rather than short-term relationships. The East Asia peoples usually regard family harmony and relationships as the foundation on which societies are organized; they therefore stress family and kinship relations when doing business. The East Asian and Arabic cultures are likely to allude to fate as an explanation for personal outcomes. They are, therefore, less likely than the Western cultures to be upset when a business deal fails to come through.

Chapter 5
The Impact of Culture on Workplace Attitudes

The culture of a society affects the values, ethics, attitudes, and assumptions of the individual. This cultural orientation also guides the individual's values, work ethics, and morality. However, basic differences exist in ethics and values of different societies.

Although the interrelationships between organizations are hinged on operational matters, more attention and resources are needed to increase understanding of the cultural differences between employees in multicultural work environments[1]. Difficulties interacting across cultures exist because in every distinct culture, beliefs, attitudes, and norms differ and are often unconsciously practiced[2]. Although, there are variations in culture within a given country, the people share common values that are used to distinguish one country's culture from another. Generally, understanding these cultural issues will assist in promoting interactions and synergies in a multicultural workplace.

Creating synergies in these interactions, however, becomes more challenging when the national cultural distance is large. National cultural distance is the degree to which the cultural norms in a country are different from those in another country[3]. These cultural differences exist in varying magnitudes and can range across values, norms, and ethics. As the national distances between the countries of the interacting individuals grow larger, the culturally-influenced issues become more challenging.

Collectivist and high power distant societies such as Saudi Arabia show much respect for authorities, titles, birth, and religious status. These cultures attach much importance to status and rank; culturally, it is important never to criticize or berate anyone in public. In contrast, such individualistic societies as the United States are achievement-oriented societies in which rewards and honor come with personal achievement. The power distance in these societies is low and hence, not much importance is attached to status and rank.

In societies with collectivist cultures, relationships play visible roles in all aspects of life, and government affairs are transacted mostly on a personal basis. That is, employment, career advancement, and organizational transactions are usually based on personal relationship. In these societies, even official interactions are friendship-based, and most often, official assistance is rendered on the basis of personal relationships. Opportunities for economic advancement also revolve around the government and its agencies and are usually dispensed through personal relationships. Paternalism is a very common leadership style in collectivist cultures where the boss is involved in such personal celebrations as weddings, children's welfare and graduation, and bereavements. The indication here is that the global manager should expect a certain level of nepotism and favoritism, especially in employment.

Chapter 6
Impact of National Culture on Organizational Cultures and Structures

The many differences in employment motivation, management styles and structure of international organizations can be traced the differences in national cultures[1]. The cultural dimensions of power distance, individualism and uncertainty avoidance have the most impacts on the culture and structure of organizations[2].

Organizational Culture

The organization culture of a company is "the taken-for-granted values and assumptions in an organization, and embodies a collective set of expectations and definitions and memories, and represents 'how things are in the organization[3]. The organizational culture and stricture of organizations are heavily influenced by the culture and other institutional environments in which they operate[4]. The institutional environments include such formal issues as economic, political and judicial rules and such informal issues as culture and ideology[5]. Organizational culture, a by-product of societal culture, in turn affects the individual's values and ethics, attitudes, assumptions and expectations[6].

The organizational members from different nationalities will tend to develop specific cultural perspectives, modifying and transforming the cultures of the organization so as to adapt them to suit their own cultural biases[7]. Sometimes it leads to different practical approaches in dealing with organizational problems. This complexity in the internal environments of international organizations leads to multiple systems of meanings and practices that coexist simultaneously[8]. The existences of these sub-cultures usually affect the operations of the organizations. Often, these sub-groups respond to the same organizational events in different ways; modifying or even ignoring the rules and procedures that emanate from the dominant organizational culture[9].

Organizational Structures

The fact that organizations are devices to distribute power as well as serve to make things more predictable, the decisive cultural dimensions in organizations are, therefore, power distance and uncertainty avoidance[10]. The large power distance and strong uncertainty avoidance of such countries as France, Latin and Mediterranean countries lead to the perception of the organization as a "pyramid of people" that should have a hierarchical bureaucratic structure[11]. The high power distance and high uncertainty avoidance cultural type of the French create the hierarchical structure of the organization that is held together by the unity of command and as well as by rules[12]. The small power distance and strong uncertainty avoidance leads the individuals in such countries as Germany, Austria, Switzerland to view the organization an order machinist, which is bureaucratic horizontal structure with least span of control[13]. The little span of control low power distance, whereas the "order of the machine" mentality reflects the adherence to rules as means of avoiding risks[14]. The small power distance and weak uncertainty avoidance of such societies as the United Kingdom, United States and Nordic countries leads to the perception of the organization as a village market" with no decisive hierarchy, flexible rules and problem resolution by negotiation that reflects small power distance and weak uncertainty avoidance[15]. These countries tend to share the perception of the organization as an adhocracy with dynamic, entrepreneurial, risk taking and innovative culture. The large power distance and the weak uncertainty avoidance of India, China and Asian countries lead to the view of the organization as an extended family with the clan/ employee focus culture[16]. Managers and organizational heads are considered parent figures but with few formal rules[17].

The most impact on organizational structures comes from the individualism, power distance and uncertainty dimensions. The cultural dimension of individualism encompasses attributes of freedom, autonomy, initiative and challenge, which are attributes that encourage decentralization. It is therefore expected that high individualism would be associated with decentralization and low individualism with centralization[18]. The high degree of centralization, which could be attributed to lack of trusts on subordinates' ability to perform, is also a reflection of the high power distance of societies[19]. One characteristic of organizations in collectivist societies is the formalization of the decision-making, communicating and controlling systems. These organizations usually practice vertical specialization where jobs are assigned to individuals but "to departments where individuals are collectively responsible for performance[20]. This would be a reflection of the collectivist culture of the society. The management system here is such that also important decisions are made at the top and is thus centralized. The organizational design adopted is usually the bureaucratic (mechanistic) design that tends to emphasize "vertical control with rigid Hierarchical relationship[21]. Here, managers have small spans of control and tend to supervise their subordinates closely.

In high power distance countries, organizations tend to use centralized decision-making process and tall organizational structures, with little or no participation of subordinates in the decision-making processes. The organizations in countries with low power distance, on the other hand, use flatter and decentralized organizational structures and smaller decision span with subordinate-centered leadership style.

Most organizations in such high power distance and high uncertainty avoidance societies as France, Belgium, Italy, Spain, Czech, Slovakia, Greece, Turkey, Japan, Korea; and the Latin American countries use vertical specialization where jobs are not assigned to individuals but "to departments where individuals are collectively responsible for performance[22]. The management system here is such that also important decisions are made at the top and is thus centralized. The organizational design is usually the bureaucratic (mechanistic) design that tends to emphasize "vertical control with rigid hierarchical relationship[23]. Here, managers have small spans of control and tend to supervise their subordinates closely. The paternalism of these systems creates a business climate where "the top man is seen as carrying the whole organization on his shoulders and enjoying it[24]. Essentially, the structure of organizations are usually highly bureaucratic and over centralized; with power and authority vested on the top management. This is attributable to acceptance of inequalities and the lack of trusts on subordinates' ability to perform.

The structure of organizations in such low to moderate power distance and weak to moderate uncertainty avoidance countries as the United States Netherlands, Norway, Canada, Australia, and New Zealand are less bureaucratic, more decentralized and more delegation of authority. The organizational designs of organizations in these societies are usually the organic and emphasize horizontal relationships, are relatively decentralized and low in specialization and formalization[25]. Formalization will be characterized by such things as organizational charts, information booklets, operating instructions, job descriptions, procedure manuals written policies, and work-flow schedules and programs[26]. Another characteristic organizational design characteristic is the horizontal specialization where individuals would be given particular functions and expected to stay in that area and develop functional expertise. The management system is usually decentralized, and decision-making pushed down the line and thus get the lower-level personnel involved.

Chapter 7
Impacts of Culture on Organizational Behavior and Management

The transferability of organizational and management planning and control systems across nations is an issue of increasing importance as movement towards globalization of business and economies continues[1]. Corporate management has come a long way from the past era of converging the principles and practices of management. The dominant belief in Europe and the United States had been that management was something universal and that there were principles of management which existed regardless of national environment and that if local or national practice deviated from these principles, it was time to change the local practices[2]. This belief in the unavoidable convergence of management practices were abandoned when it became apparent that nationalities held unto their cultures and those cultures play a dominant role in management.

Cultures and nationalities are important because we all derive our identities from them and our thinking is partly conditioned by our culture. Certain working practices are, therefore, not only culture-bound but also vary with cultures. The tendencies of any human system as defined by their cultural dimensions, therefore, have profound influences on personal and organizational practices. Such practices include tendencies to plan or act on ad-hoc basis, personal or group achievement-driven goals, job satisfaction, commitment and decision-making processes.

The global business environment demands good understanding of cultural diversity[3]. This is because national culture has been found to have greater impact on employees that the organizational of the business entity[4]. National culture can influence managerial decision-making, leadership style and management practices[5].

Organizational culture, a by-product of societal culture, affects the individual's values and ethics, attitudes, assumptions and expectations[6]. Cultures influence organizational behavior because, firstly, employees bring their customs and languages to work. Secondly, the organizational culture, which, is built on its home culture affects the values, ethics, attitudes, and expectations of the employees. Essentially, therefore, once the individual is within the sphere of influence of the organization, such individual becomes affected, not only by his or her national culture, but also by the culture of the organization. Such mixing of societal and organizational cultures creates the dynamics and complexities of multicultural workplaces that have become the hallmarks in multinational organizations. Management attitudes and practices are, therefore, culture bound[7].

In organizational behavior and management, the decisive cultural dimensions are power distance, uncertainty avoidance and masculinity. In decision-making processes, cultural orientation determines how quickly and how analytically a decision could be made. Members from cultural systems with individualistic orientation are usually quick in making decisions but without detailed analysis. This is because decision-making is carried out by individual managers. In these individualistic societies, promotions are usually based on achievement and salaries based on market value.

On the other hand, decisions making by members from systems with collectivist orientation are usually slow but likely to be more detailed in analysis. This is because decision-making is usually carried out be groups. Organizations in individualistic societies are more likely to encourage individual initiative. Those in collectivist countries are less likely to encourage individual initiative; and salaries and promotions are based on seniority.

The organizations in high individualized as United States, Canada, Australia, and Germany support personal responsibility and personal performance evaluation. In contrast, the societies that are low in individualism (collectivist) as Korea, Japan, Philippines, Mexico, Brazil, and Thailand, job designed are team-based with group goals and group performance evaluation. Family tiers and personal relationships are major determinants of most job recruitments in these societies; and often, there is family and community influence on senior managers to employ as far as possible, their own kith and kin[8].

The strict adherence to planning as an imperative organizational practice is related to the uncertainty avoidance dimension of culture[9]. The attitudes towards fate and preoccupation with the immediate are indications of weak uncertainty avoidance societies and this characteristic, militates against strategic planning, which requires consideration for the future[10]. Therefore, whereas human systems with high uncertainty avoidance culture as Iran, China, Mexico, and Italy, usually insist on proper and detailed planning, those with low uncertainty avoidance orientation as the Nordic countries have the tendency to operate on an ad-hoc basis. Although the Asians are collectivist, the Confucian orientation of the East Asians cultures (China, Philippines, Hong Kong, Malaysia, Singapore, Taiwan, Indonesia, South Vietnam, and Thailand) endows them with a long-term orientation. This long-term orientation brings about a focus on the future.

Organizations in high uncertainty avoidance societies are also more likely to emphasize security of job tenure, appreciate experts and their knowledge, and have more written rules and procedures, less risk taking by managers. These organizations tend to have bureaucratic rules and are usually hierarchical; trusting only family and friend to handles important assignment. Employees in high uncertainty avoidance societies prefer structured situations where rules of conduct and decision making are clearly documented[11]. In low uncertainty avoidance societies, organizations are more willing to accept risks associated with the unknown, fewer written rules and procedures, more risks taking by managers, more ambitious employees, and higher employee turn-over. Organizations in these societies avoid hierarchy, and generally consider such inefficient and counterproductive.

In high power distance societies, organizations accept

outward show of power as protocol, chain command, and respect for existing hierarchy. In high power distance societies, employees are comfortable receiving commands from superiors; and resolving conflicts through formal rules and authority[12]. In these organizations, rewards and redress of grievances are usually at the direction of the power holders, rather than corporate procedures. Organizations in low power distance societies tend to value competence over seniority.

In low power distance societies, subordinates and superiors regard each other as like (or equivalent) people, who have equal rights[13], and subordinates expect to be consulted on decisions or actions that affect them[14]. Employees prefer being involved in decisions, resolving conflicts through personal networks and coalitions[15]. By contrast, in high power distance societies, superiors are expected to lead, to make decisions autocratically and paternalistically, and subordinates are generally afraid and unwilling to disagree with their superiors[16].

Employees in organizations in countries with high power distance, workers are more likely to obey the orders of their superiors and are less likely to question authority. Whereas, in low power distance societies, workers are more likely to question their bosses, and participative management is more likely to be used.

The low power distance cultures as Demark, Netherlands and the United States prefer consultation and participation whereas the high distance cultures as Russian, Thailand and Spain prefer autocratic and are reluctant to trust subordinates. The High power distance societies such as Russian, Thailand and Spain, China make a distinction people with status and power and people without it.

The typical management style in societies with high power distance and high uncertainty avoidance does not encourage employee involvement in decision-making and "within business organizations, there appears to be little participation among employees[17]. Organizations will need to adjust its control structures in order to be able to ally across cultures.

Some studies have also indicated that employees from systems with high power distance and collectivist orientation are likely to resist any practices of corporate self-management. This is because, people are more likely to resist self-management if they dislike stepping outside the bonds of authority, working autonomously, and taking initiatives[18]. Such attitudes are likely to be held by those high on measured power distance, which is characterized by a belief in the importance of status and power differences.

In like manner, systems with high masculine orientation operate with an aggressive and achievement-driven organizational and supervisory style. For example, a culture of emphasis on achievement, assertiveness, and material success may be appropriate for the United States. This tendency could, however, create some measure of concern for many other international environments. Often it brings resentment and becomes counterproductive. In high masculinity societies, workers place more importance on earnings, recognition, advancement, challenge and wealth. Workers in these societies also experience higher job stress. In high femininity (low masculinity) societies, workers place great importance on cooperation, employment security, and friendly work environment. Here, workers tend to experience less work stress.

Given these differences, diversity, if properly managed, especially in task-oriented assignments, creates such advantages as creativity, innovative ideas, and minimal groupthink. For people serving abroad, the most important aspects of multicultural relationships are their effects on attitudes and communication.

Chapter 8
Impacts of Culture on Work Teams

Individuals bring cultures of origin and national cultures to work[1]. National cultures explain between 25% to 50% variations in altitudes which reflect in such social behaviors as aggression, conflict resolution, social interactions, dominance, conformity, and obedience[2]. This national culture also explains the same level of variations in such organizational behaviors as decision-making and leadership behaviors[3].

In today's penchant for the pursuit of global integration in business, philanthropy, and intergovernmental relationship, different cultures interact; thereby creating much higher levels of cultural diversity in workplaces. Organizations operating or expanding globally to tap the potential of the foreign markets use multicultural teams because of their capacities for flexibility, responsiveness, and improved source utilization[4]. The variety of perspectives, skills and other personal attributes are some of the benefits derivable from multicultural teams[5].

The major trend today is that organizations and companies are now accepting the fact that these differences enable them competes globally and also acquire rich sources of new talents. The heterogeneity of team members leads to teams having visionaries, communicators, catalysts and doers all together, especially when each member plays an adhesive role in sustaining team cohesiveness and effectiveness[6].

This cultural diversity, however can lead to a unique set of challenges as people from these different cultures interact. Resulting from the different perceptions of values and environment; communication styles, work ethics and motives; and issues of ethnocentrism and prejudices; multicultural work teams are usually vulnerable to interaction problems[7].

In these global organizations, it is quite common for an employee to born into a culture that is distinctively different from the one in which he or she works or interacts with. Managing the cultural differences and conflicts have, therefore become a common challenge of multicultural work teams[8]. The situation is made more imperative because while most organizations and professions have codified set of ethical rules, cultures do not. Hence, it is important to understand the ethical values of the different cultures one interacts with. Most organizations have recognized the diverse nature of the workplace, and have increasingly focused on multicultural team units[9]. This is because; diversifying the workforce can improve team performance and advance organizational effectiveness[10].

Unlike members of the same cultural type who tend to share similar opinions and beliefs, working towards a feeling of harmonious interdependence as intercultural relationship is established, multicultural work teams come with differences in values and beliefs[11]. Managing a same-culture team would obviously be easier because they share common language, values and understanding and would thus have better interpersonal relationship and communication. Hence, with a same-culture team, it is easier to create a workplace synergy.

When managing the workforce of multicultural organizations, however, both the societal and organizational cultures have to be taken into consideration. To work effectively, therefore, multicultural team members need to know and appreciate the cultural orientation of the others[12]. Obviously national cultures have impacts on the performance of multicultural teams[13]. The two key cultural dimensions that are most likely to influence teamwork are power distance, uncertainty avoidance and individualism/collectivism.

Cultural considerations even exist on the perception of work teams[14]. Team members from individualistic societies tend to construct work teams as project teams whose activity is limited to the time during the team works on the project. The collectivist team members, on the other hand, tend to view work teams as more like a family whose activity is broad, extending to other domains of life[15].

Work team members from individualistic societies such as United States, Germany, and Hungary value autonomy, self- interest and performance. They are, therefore, more likely to be more task-focused, and hence less responsive to non-task leadership orientation. The individuals from this cultural dimension are likely to view group membership as task-specific and transitory[16].

Team members from collectivist societies, on the other hand, are likely to view work team member as long term and more far reaching. Collectivist cultures exhibit more dependence on teams, more conforming, more team-oriented[17]. These societies, such as Japan, Sweden, and Russia, value harmony and cooperation[18]. Work team members from collectivist societies are, therefore, more responsive to charismatic leadership that emphasizes vision and emotions.

Also, work teams with collectivist orientations tend to behave more cooperatively, have fewer conflicts, and develop more cooperating tactics and less competitive tactics[19]. Conversely, individualistic oriented person will regard a team as a task-oriented entity that should have defined roles and deliverables, and hence mostly concerned with performance and accomplishment of specific objectives[20].

Collectivist oriented individuals tend to be more inclined to the self-effectiveness of teamwork and team-based rewards. This is because collectivist individuals have a concept of teamwork that is broader and less task-focused. In the collectivist teams, individuals are to eat and socialize together as a logical extension of their life within the organization. Multicultural teams whose members differ in cultural orientation of individualism and collectivist are, therefore, likely to have challenges that border on team roles and processes because of the underlying differences in the senses of personal and organizational responsibility[21].

Work teams from low power distance cultures tend toward consultation, participation, and practicality[22]. Such cultures with low power distance are more likely to minimize inequalities, have less autocratic leadership, and favor less centralization of authority. Work teams in such societies prefer to resolve conflicts more through personal networks and coalitions[23]. Such low power distance cultures as Denmark, The Netherlands and the United States tend to be more egalitarian and they also prefer participatory decision making.

In contrast, those cultures, high in power distance, accept autocratic or majority rule decision-making, and are reluctant to trust anyone other than friends and relatives[24]. Work teams from cultures high in power distance, are more likely to accept inequalities, and authoritarian leadership. In these societies, work teams are comfortable to resolve conflicts through formal rues and authority. Such high power distance societies as Russia, Thailand, and Spain consider power and status when dealing with others. When there is significant differences in power distance between members, difficulties may occur on the acceptable communication and leadership patterns[25].

The low uncertainty avoidance cultures such as Russia, Greece, and Venezuela demand less structure and are not much concerned about following rules and procedures. In such societies, work teams prefer that the rules of conduct and decision making are clearly documented. The high uncertainty avoidance cultures such as Sweden, Germany, and the moderate United States prefer consistence, structured procedures, and expectations[26].

Individuals with long-term perspective culture and high uncertainty avoidance such as the Chinese are likely to be comfortable with long-term planning and with the continuous evaluation processes of management. Trying to build a cultural bonding with this individual may entail giving such individuals responsibilities that involve planning and monitoring. Obviously, today's successful businesses feel uncomfortable with uncertainty. Strict adherence and easy acceptance of planning as an imperative business practice is related to the uncertainty avoidance dimension of culture. Human systems with high uncertainty avoidance culture usually insist on proper and detailed planning while systems with low uncertainty avoidance orientation usually operate on ad-hoc basis. Hence, building workplace synergies with individuals that have tolerance for the unpredictable could be difficult. This would definitely be one aspect where the individual has to be re-programmed to adapt to the new culture of supporting beliefs that assure certainty and conformity.

Typically, in high individualistic and low power distance societies as Australia, managers create job-based work designs that hinge on individual initiative and responsibility. Conversely, in collectivist and high power distance countries as China, managers prefer team-based work groups with strong oversight functions and controls by supervisors

Cultural Competence for multicultural team members

The main purposes of team building are to set goals, to allocate work performance, to examine group processes and to examine the relationships among people doing the work[27]. Multicultural teams are, therefore, task-oriented groups that consist of people of different national cultures[28]. The goal should be to develop global teams that are capable of overcoming cultural biases and working together in an efficient and harmonious manner[29]. To achieve this, individual team members must acquire the necessary cross-cultural communication competence cross-cultural conflict management abilities; have the willingness to seek clarification, and ability to build trust and interpersonal relationships.

Cross-cultural Communications Competence

Communication is one of the major tools for the management of an organization or work team. Communication is usually most effective when communicators share common values and understanding. In a multicultural work teams, however, creating effective communication could be challenging the lack of effective communication is likely to be a barrier. More often than not, this would lead to mistrust which could lead to workplace conflicts.

Cross cultural communication accounts for about 20% of the variance in performance level of multicultural work teams[30]. The performance of a multicultural work team will, therefore, depend on how well the team members work with each. Cross cultural communication competence increases the likelihood of high team performance because team members will better understand their colleagues[31]. Cross cultural communication competence, therefore, improves the decision-making and problem-solving abilities of team members[32]. The cross cultural communication competence of a multicultural team member would, therefore, determine his or her ability to perform an assigned task effectively.

The internationalization of businesses, therefore, requires managers to become conscious of communications procedures and conventions of foreign and diverse number of cultures. In today's world, national boundaries are constantly and societies are moving towards greater interdependency and interconnectedness[33]. The propensity of this increasing globalization poses unique challenges to the issue of how people from diverse cultural backgrounds attempt to effectively communicate on daily basis[34]. The cross cultural communication competence of the team members will help them to overcome the many challenges that usually face multicultural work teams[35]. The characteristics that constitute cross cultural communication competence include both relational and communications skills[36]. This competence, however, entails not only the knowledge of the culture and language, it also entails the ability to communicate empathy, human warmth, and appreciate anxiety and uncertainty[37].

Navigating conflicts

Cultural problems arise from differences in behavior, thinking, assumptions and values between people of different nationalities. A deeper understanding of the nature of the cultural differences will increase effectiveness in cross-cultural situations[38]. The awareness that differences in cultural values and beliefs, communication styles, and approaches to decision-making, problem solving, and conflict resolution tends to help team members in overcoming the problems posed by cultural differences. A favorable disposition towards learning about other cultures helps in the establishment of rapport among team members. Communication is one of the most effective tools for managing a multicultural work team. There are a lot of issues involved in this kind of cross-cultural communication and these issues in one way or the other impact on the work of the committee. Overall, if this diversity is not properly managed, it could lead to a lack of communication that could disrupt cohesion among the team members.

Cross-cultural Conflict management abilities

Usually, it is often challenging to work with persons from different cultural background. The approaches to project management tasks such as scheduling, goal setting, task assignment and leadership differ across cultures require that teams develop good relationships so that they can bridge any existing differences[39].

Team members from individualistic societies are likely to accept conflict management and resolution strategies that entails the discussion of the issues even if it creates open disagreement because getting to the bottom of the issue is critical to the job performance[40]. This orientation would be at variance with those the individuals from the collectivist societies in which "group and strong relationships among the members of the group are seen as the key to high performance[41].

In conflict resolutions, team members should have a plan to deal with cultural clashes as the team begins working from different perspectives to achieve common objectives. These cultural differences would always be a source of conflicts and dilemmas. The challenge is to search for new ways to understand the different value systems involved and reinforced through traditions, as well as ways to minimize the gap between the cultural differences[42]. A way to minimize the problems that can arise from these dilemmas is an accurate assessment of the cultures in relationship to the perception and handling of conflicts. The Anglo-Saxon and the Nordic group tend to relish in the conflict handling styles of dominating or compromising while the Arabic, Asian, Latin and Indian group tend to prefer the obliging or avoiding style to preserve relationships. Team leaders are better advised to use, the integrative (problem-solving) style of conflict resolution that tends to deal with the underlying problem rather than the symptoms.

Although it has been argued that a conflict can be made productive when it leads to resolution and to a new understanding of how the parties can mutually achieve joint needs. To a large extent, creativity is impossible without conflict; by the same token, without creativity as a goal, conflict becomes dysfunctional[43]. Hence, the end goal of conflicts resolutions should be creation of new understanding and new opportunities.

Willingness to seek Clarifications

Effective communication in a multicultural team occurs when team members hear what was intended to be said[44]. Communication is probably one of the most relevant tools for managing a multicultural organization. Every management function involves some form of direct or indirect communication[45]. Effective communication in a multicultural organization is an imperative because it improves decision making. Team members should, therefore, always be willing to seek clarifications whenever in doubt[46].

Ability to build trust and interpersonal relationship

To communicate effectively across cultures, team members need to develop intercultural sensitivity, trust and good relationships[47]. The key to gaining trust is by having an open mind and be willing to listen to others. Being open-minded, respectful and patient in dealing with differences made a difference in communicating across cultures[48]. Mistrust sometimes constitutes a barrier to effective communication and where such exists must be overcome by creating trust and credibility.

Chapter 9
Impacts of Culture on Organizational Leadership

Culture is a system of shared meaning where members of the same culture have a common way of viewing events and objects.[1] This culture is inherently tied to leadership behaviors[2] and is therefore, central to international management.[3] Leadership is a major component of the social fabric of many organizations.[4] Cultural background does have an influence on leadership behaviors.[5] Differences in leadership behaviors are therefore, expected in societies that differ in cultural orientation.[6] The cultural diversity of employees in multicultural organizations presents substantial challenges to organizational leadership. Given the increasing globalization and interdependence among nations, the need for better understanding of cultural influences on organizational leadership continues to grow.[7] Moreover, organizational leadership behaviors are the ability of an individual to influence, motivate, and enable others to contribute toward the effectiveness and success of an organization of which they are members[8].

Leadership behaviors differ in societies that have different cultural profiles[9]. These differences in cultural background characteristics usually results in different leadership behaviors, such as use of power and supervision[10]. Moreover, studies commissioned under the auspices of Global Leadership and Organizational Behavior Effectiveness (GLOBE) has shown that leadership behaviors are significantly closely associated with cultural background[11].

A leadership that adopts an autocratic style may be more accepted and effective in a high power distance culture as China than a low power distance culture as Australia.

Managers that work in foreign settings ought to recognize that notions of what constitutes ideal leadership behaviors vary from culture to culture[12]. For instance, in such high power distance cultures as China that value decisiveness and hierarchy, leaders might prefer autocratic styles with the subordinates offering their loyalty and obedience. In contrasts, in such cultures as Canadian and Australian, that value egalitarianism, leader might prefer to be consultative, with the subordinates challenging and speaking their minds.

The perceptions of the leadership, which is cultural oriented, is what the followers act on, thereby impacting the outcome of the leadership process[13]. The cultural values of a society could determine whether specific leadership characteristics and styles acceptable and effective[14]. Although the findings of the GLOBE research program indicate that such positive leadership attitudes as vision, intelligence, trustworthiness and decisiveness are universally endorsed, such others as compassion, dominance, orderliness and risk taking are culturally contingent[15]. In some cultures a leader might may to take strong decisive unilateral actions to be seen as a leader, whereas some other cultures might prefer democratic approaches[16]. Global managers who work in foreign environments need to recognize that the notions of what constitutes leadership vary from culture to culture[17]. To perform effectively, therefore, global managers need to be aware of the cultural differences and similarities in leadership. Autocratic leadership characteristics are essentially reflective of the high power distance of the society[18].

The most relevant cultural dimensions to organizational leadership are individualism and power distance. Leadership in individualistic societies is based on the presumed needs of individuals who ultimately seek their self-interest[19]. The leadership approach is, however, participative, with the leaders encouraging the employees to play active roles in assuming control of their work processes. Leadership in collectivist societies on the other hand, is a group phenomenon[20]. Leadership in organizations in such societies is a group phenomenon and collective responsibility. Moreover, individuals in collectivist societies bring loyalty to their jobs; while expecting protection from their leaders/employers. The approach to leadership in these societies is usually either paternalistic or autocratic.

In organizations, the level of power distance is closely related to the degree of centralization of authority and the degree of autocratic leadership[21]. In countries with small power distances, such as the United States, the other Anglo- countries, the Nordic, and the Germanic countries, although the initiative belongs to the leader, subordinates are usually allowed to participate in the decision making process[22]. In high power distance societies as France and Belgium subordinates do not usually participate, rather the expectation is that the leader leads autocratically without inputs from the subordinates who are simply obey orders and instructions[23]. In these countries, there is very little participative leadership[24]. If however, such high power distance were also collectivist as in Asian and African countries, subordinates could indirectly participate by influencing the leader or other participants who are expectedly also members the in-group.

In the low power distance countries as Denmark, Sweden or Israel, subordinates, do necessarily wait until the boss takes the initiatives before participating in the management decision-making processes and there are no management prerogatives that are automatically accepted[25]. Employees in these societies usually support any codetermination in which individuals or their groups can take initiatives toward organizational management[26].

Autocratic leadership is likely to be more acceptable and effective for organizations in such high distance cultures as China, Saudi Arabia, Iran, Turkey, Malaysia, Indonesia, Thailand, and India than low power distance cultures as Australia, Switzerland, Sweden, Finland and Netherlands. In low power distance societies, subordinates, and superiors perceive and treat each other as likes with equal rights, and subordinates expect to have inputs in the decisions or actions affecting them[27]. These tend to create a situation in which the leadership styles in such societies are usually participatory. By contrasts, in high power distance societies, superiors expect to lead, make decisions either autocratically or paternalistically, and the subordinates are generally afraid and unwilling to disagree with their superiors[28].

In organizations, the degree of autocratic leadership is rooted in the mindset of, not only those in powers, but also in those at the bottom of the hierarchy. The first step towards the leadership of the team is to appreciate that there is a major relationship between the cultural orientation of any human being and his/her working and business practices. In international organizations, differences in culture also manifest in differences in the use power and supervision of subordinates[29]. Organizations in high power distance countries are most likely to use coercive powers and close supervision of subordinates; whereas those in low distance societies are more likely to use participative powers structures and loose spans of controls. The autocratic leadership characteristics of African organizations reflect the high power distance of most African societies[30].

Wielding Power in Strange Lands

Power is the potential ability to influence the behavior of others. Power represents the resources with which a leader effects changes in employee behavior. Leaders often use their powers to affect the behavior of subordinates. The ability of leadership to influence people to direct their efforts towards the achievement of some particular goal or goals are derivable from the power such a leader exercises.

Although one party may be more dependent than the other, a relationship exists only when each party has something of value to offer to the other[31]. Hence, some interdependence exists between the parties; with the individuals over whom power is exercised having a counter-power. For instance, a manager may exercise control due to his or her power to retain and promote a subordinate. However, the subordinate does exercise a measure of control through the counter-power that arises from his or her ability to work more productively or less; which in turn would have a positive or negative effect on the manager's job performance evaluation. It is this counter power that somewhat compels managers to use their power judiciously so as not to upset this relationship[32].

In high power distance societies, managers tend to use coercive power, demanding total obedience, and applying sanctions for noncompliance. In societies with low power distance, although individuals accept that leaders have the right to exert influence over them, leaders still accept the efficacy of participation by others. In these societies power is perceived as a mutual interaction between the individual that exercises power and the individuals or groups over whom power is exercised. Although the initiatives and final decisions rest on the leader, subordinates are allowed to participate in the decision making process.

In these low power distance societies, managers also tend toward delegating powers to subordinates. Delegation is the process granting decision making authority to lower-level employees[33]. Delegation makes the job of the manager easier, while at same giving lower-level employees a "sense of belonging" in the organization. Hence, the positive outcome of delegation of power is employee empowerment. Empowerment as the act of recognizing and releasing into the organization, the power that employees already have by virtue of their knowledge, experience and internal motivation[34].

Empowerment entails the involvement of members of staff at every level in the decision-making process; which in turn allows such organization to tap into the creativity and energy of the employees. This will in turn, create more positive feeling about work and the organization, more job satisfaction, and greater commitment to the organization. Hence, key element of empowerment is pushing decision-making progressively down to lower levels[35]. By empowering employees; the total effective power of the organization seems to increase. This is because everybody would have more say, and hence, contribute more to the organizational goals. Organizations should view power as a process rather than a position; and one way to create that process is through the delegation of power.

Chapter 10
Impacts of Culture on International Negotiations

As an organization increases it oversea transactions, the frequency of discussions and negotiations across countries and cultures increase. Negotiation, in itself, is a special communication task that occurs when two parties, not only have common interests that should enable them to work together, but also have conflicting interest that could prevent them from working together[1]. Negotiation behaviors differ from one culture to the other[2]. Unless already culturally attuned, negotiators are usually more likely to assess attitudes and communications through their own cultural lens. This is because, no matter the strategies the intercultural partners bring to the table, they are bound to be different because their cultures have different priorities and values. The first steps toward successful international negotiation is recognizing and appreciating that the other party is different in motivation, perception, beliefs and expectations. It is the culture that tells them what is important, enables then assign meanings and motives to the other side's communication.

These cultural diversities can lead to unique sets of challenges as people from these different cultural backgrounds interact. Moreover, the diversities also create risks of misunderstanding, which may hamper the collaboration between interacting partners or negotiators. Differences in culture between the negotiating groups can create, not only misunderstandings in communication, but also difficulties in interpreting actions. The ever present issue in international negotiations, therefore, is the difference of culture between the parties. The knowledge of the other party's cultures, therefore, enables you communicate, understand and anticipate more effectively. These cultural diversities can, however, lead to unique sets of challenges as people from these different cultural backgrounds interact. Moreover, the diversities also create risks of misunderstanding, which may hamper the collaboration between interacting partners or negotiators.

A negotiation between parties with similar cultural orientations usually involves fewer conflicts because the two negotiators will rely on their common culture to interpret each other's statements and actions. When, however, persons from two different cultures negotiate, they rely on different cultural orientations to interpret each other's statements and actions. Understanding different cultures helps to create strategies for communicating and negotiating with people from such cultures. When negotiation in individualistic societies, decisions are often made on the spot without further consultations; and when there is a deadlock, such is resolved by voting. In contrast to this, negotiations in communitarian societies are often carried out by teams that do not usually take the ultimate decisions. The negotiating team usually consults with superior groups, which usually reach decisions by consensus.

In individualistic societies, tasks usually prevail over relationships[3]. Moreover, establishing rapport does not usually go beyond the exchange of business cards. These individualistic cultures, placing emphasis on achievement, doing and accomplishing goals tend to look upon negotiations as win situations that entail not having to make concessions beyond the pre-set bargaining limits. Organizations in these societies tend to linear logics in negotiations, stressing specifics over generalities. Members from these societies expect the other side to be empowered enough as to make decisions with further reference to nonparticipating individuals. Business people from such individualistic countries as the United States and Finland rely on contracts to enforce commitments; whereas those from collectivist cultures as Turkey and Mexico will rely on relationship between the two parties[4]. In negotiations, assumptions or issues that may be taken as self-evident must be stated explicitly in individualistic cultures[5]. For this culture, the essence of negotiation is a binding contract that arises from either a 'win' negotiating attitude. Negotiations are, therefore competitive, and in some cases, confrontational.

In collectivist cultures, relationships must be established between two parties before they can do business[6]. In these societies, personal relationships usually prevail over task considerations[7]. Although people from collectivist societies (Mexico) will base trust on relationship rather than contract, such trust is usually reserved members of their in-group, their relatives or those with whom a relationship has been established[8]. The collectivist cultures as Arabs and Chinese value relationships, because they believe that, with it, comes harmony and obligations. These societies tend to stress general agreements over specific issues, believing that details can be worked out in future[9]. The collectivist societies tend to use more solution-oriented strategies than the individualistic societies that are usually prone toward control. In these cultures, the need for building and sustaining relationships that last longer that the lifetime of the negotiators are emphasized to create win-win situations. For this culture, the essence of negotiating is to build lasting relationships, arising from win-win negotiating attitude. Negotiations in these cultures therefore tend toward the display of harmonious relationship.

In negotiations, the low risk avoidance societies, namely, Denmark, Sweden, Great Britain, India, and Singapore usually require less information, have less people in decision-making, and can act quickly[10]. The high risk avoidance societies as Germany, Portugal, France, Spain, Mexico and Belgium, on the other hand, tend to lots of bureaucratic rules, rely on standards and formulas, or trust only family and friends.

Organizations in cultures with low uncertainty avoidance have fewer people involved in negotiations, and can, therefore, act more quickly than the high uncertainty avoidance societies. The high uncertainty avoidance tendencies usually lead to the hoarding of information that could hinder overall interest and creative proposals.

In cultures with high power distance, ultimate authority is more likely to lie with someone who is not even present at the negotiating table. Where the society is collectivist and also have a high power distance, the decision-maker may be at the table without giving such prominence up. Among the Arabs, for instance, the person who asks the most questions in business negotiations is likely to be the least important. The key decision-maker is likely to merely listen and observe. Individuals from high power distance usually have low faith in people who are not friends or family members[11].

Feminine (low masculinity) cultures such as Finland and Turkey tend towards mutually beneficial outcomes in negotiations. These countries usually adopt the integrative approach to negotiations. In masculine societies where competitiveness and assertiveness are profound, the individuals will likely perceive negotiation in win-lose terms[12]. Low masculinity and low power distance positively relate to sharing information, which enables the creativity in offering proposals that could lead to integrative negotiation attitudes. The Confucian undertone of the East Asian culture proposes moderation and avoidance of acts or tactics that are capable of destroying harmony. The need to build relationships and harmony, therefore, also influences the negotiation tactics of these nations.

A relative comparison of the negotiating styles of American and Chinese shows that the Chinese (as with the Japanese and other Asian cultures) often consider the goal of negotiation, not as a signed contract, but the creation of relationship[13]. For Americans, signing a contract is closing a deal; for the Chinese it is the opening of a relationship[14]. Americans, therefore, prefer detailed contracts that aim to anticipate all possible circumstances and eventualities. The Chinese prefer the general principles; any unexpected circumstances will be dealt with on the basis of an existing relationship and not on the basis of a contract[15]. Americans also tend to follow the approach of having a leader who has complete authority to decide all matter; whereas the Chinese stress team negotiations and consensus decision-making.

The explosion of global trades and interactions has, however, increased relationship sensitivities in individualistic cultures as well as contract sensitivities in collectivist cultures. The important goal is for the manager involved in international negotiations to realize that contracts and relationships can exist mutually by complimenting each other[16].

Chapter 11
Impacts of Culture on International Alliances and Joint Ventures

Joint ventures are legally and economically distinct organizational entities created by two or more parent organizations that collectively invest capital and other resources to pursue strategic objectives[1]. The global economy is, however, a rich mix of cultures, with different ideas, different ways of social conduct and different methods of organizing work[2]. In a global alliance, when a great deal of differences between the national cultures of the two companies and hence there are bound to be some areas of conflict. Studies of mergers indicated that they frequently failed due to incompatible cultures[3].

The primary consideration for establishing a business is the availability of attractive market opportunities. Others include the advancement of the financial sectors, reliable legal systems, and political stability. The expected cultural orientation of the country would be considered since this is likely to determine the degree of fit between the parent company and its subsidiaries. This is because the degree of homogeneity between the foreign subsidiary and the parent corporation is a significant factor[4]. International business is the life blood of many of today's enterprises and brings executives into face-to-face contact with other executives of totally different cultural backgrounds[5]. These cultural differences often create misunderstanding, leading to ineffectiveness in face-to-face interactions[6]. It has become evident that persons of dissimilar cultures are having more difficulties communicating effectively than they are with those from the same cultures[7]. The form a company takes and the organizational structure is chosen to support it will have a substantial impact on the firm's success [8]. The cultural dimensions of power distance and uncertainty avoidance are the two most important dimensions of culture in organizations[9].

The organizational cultures of firms are heavily influenced by the culture and other institutional environments in which they operate[10]. When businesses and organizations embark on joint ventures, there could be organizational changes arising from conflicts and distortions in the two different styles of management. However, there would also be a need to take the various individual into cognizance because organizational changes are unlikely to succeed if it is based on a set of values that is highly inconsistent with employees' individual values[11].

Cross-cultural alliances, acquisitions and mergers create the need to work out differences where ethical values differ. Cultural diversity can lead to a unique set of challenges when people from different cultures interact. Granted that organizations are prone to carry their home practices with them as they move into foreign markets[12], it is important to understand the ethical values of the different cultures. While most businesses have codified set of ethical rules, cultures do not. In the global organization, it is quite common for an employee to be from a different culture from the one in which he or she is operating. The ethical standpoint of the employee who represents the interest of the business in a particular culture becomes of utmost importance.

Although alliances and joint ventures can be attractive, they can equally expose organizations to risks that arise from the conflicts involved in molding two cultures into one. Some of these risks, however, can be mitigated if the cultural orientations of the allying organizations are taken into consideration during such alliances or joint ventures. Although integration between companies must be based on operational matters; more attention and resources need to be given to cultural differences between partners[13].

The management of alliances and joint between organizations that domicile in countries with large national cultural distance can be quite challenging. National cultural distance could be defines as "the degree to which the cultural norms in one country are different from those in another country"[14]. When the home country has both high power distance and high uncertainty avoidance, authority is likely to be "vested in higher levels in the organizations and an authoritarian management style would be quite acceptable"[15], and employees would generally be willing to adhere to managerial control[16].

Organizations from collectivist cultures are more likely than those from individualistic cultures to select a joint venture instead of a wholly owned investment vehicle[17]. Organizations in specific cultures as the United States are more likely to emphasize shareholders' value whereas those in such diffused culture as France, Germany and China .are more holistic and tend to emphasize stakeholders' values[18]. Hence, an alliance involving diffused cultures would be better off concentrating on the benefits accruing to all the stakeholders.

Joint venture investments between such ascription cultures as Taiwan and Mexico could sometimes create conflict because people may be in positions of authority because of who they are or who their family is, and they cannot be removed from that position even when they do not achieve desired results[19].

Cultural competence Steps for Successful Alliances and Joint Ventures

The overall vision of the alliance must be translated into strategy and plan of action. First and foremost, the question is, how will the operations and resources of the two companies be integrated be integrated in such a way as to achieve the necessary synergies? To manage a cross cultural joint venture or business alliance, the allying organization must conduct cultural due diligence, offer Alliance training to concerned staff, develop mechanism for dealing with multicultural conflicts.

Conducting Cultural Due Diligence

A cultural due diligence must be conducted to determine the cultural compatibility of the allying partners. A way to minimize the problems that can arise from these dilemmas is an accurate assessment of the organizational culture[20]. These conflicts would always arise. The 'cultural audit' of the partner would include the evaluation of the partner's communication style, control mechanism, compensation orientation, recruitment policies and the corporate reward system of the company.

Developing Mechanism for Cross cultural Conflict Management

The allying organizations should have a plan to deal with cultural clashes as their employees and executives begin working from different perspectives to achieve common objectives of the new entity. These cultural differences would always be a source of conflicts and dilemmas. However, the tasks of the management are to ensure that the conflicts do not become dysfunctional. The challenge is to search for new ways to understand the different value systems involved and reinforced through traditions, as well as ways to minimize the gap between the cultural differences[21].

Developing shared organizational culture

One way to cope is to foster a distinct and shared culture inside the alliance that could ease tensions between partners, building an atmosphere of responsibility for the results of the partnership[22]. This is because a work group becomes a team when leadership becomes a shared activity[23]. Hence, to build a team by through shared organizational culture, it would be necessary to help the team members learn about the cross-cultural differences and similarities between themselves and their new colleagues. For example, an alliance between German and Japanese companies would find such common grounds as respect for punctuality and the development of clear and detailed agendas. In addition, each group has to be taught to avoid corporate ethnocentrism by learning that 'the way we do things here', may not necessarily be the best, and is definitely not 'the way they do things over there'. For a multicultural organization to function at its optimal capacity there must be cultural synergy among its staff.

Alliance Training

Alliance training is a necessary tool of the competence training required by the employees that would be involved in the alliance. This would always open up a window of learning opportunities for the employees as they would be constantly required to deal with persons and issues outside their culture. Alliance training is therefore, a good and relatively inexpensive way to foster the alliance integration process is to open up in-house training to staff in the alliance unit and when appropriate, to those from the partner[24].

Recognition and Respect for partner's culture

Managers should be trained recognize the existence of cultural differences between the partners and learn to respect, accept and understand those differences. Recognizing the implicit beliefs in a society, respecting them, and reconciling them, are the keys to successful alliances[25]. The recognition and respect for the cultures of the allying partners is a necessary step. The goal of this respect and recognition is to build a cultural synergy through the reconciliation of the cultural differences. This will promote and encourage behaviors that would allow the interaction of contrasting values because, "without reconciliation, people run the risk of supporting stereotypical views of culture[26].

The respect for the partner's needs and mutual value creation are also prerequisites for a successful relationship. This success must be measurable. However, the appropriate measure depends on the objective of the alliance, remembering that objectives typically change as the alliance evolves[27]. Being open-minded, respectful and patient in dealing with differences made a difference in communicating across cultures[28]. Mistrust sometimes constitutes a barrier to effective communication and where such exists must be overcome by creating trust and credibility.

Cross cultural Communication competence training

Cultural difference often create misunderstanding, leading to ineffectiveness in face-to-face interactions[29]. The essence of communication competence training would be to sensitize the workers as to the differences is cultural orientation and culture-dependent differences in attitudes, values and work styles and communication styles. This communication competence is essentially the ability to apply language skills to situations, thereby making good use of communication to effectively attain goals[30].

Chapter 12
Rules of Thumbs for Managing Across Cultures

The main cultural variables that affect one's ability to function effectively abroad are communication, perception, and cultural barriers[1]. Communication is the process of transferring meanings from sender to receiver[2]. Miscommunication therefore occurs when messages are not received or not correctly decoded. The various issues that can cause miscommunication include the differing styles of communication, trouble with accents, and language fluency[3]. Miscommunication, misunderstandings, and misperceptions can impair the free flow of ideas. Therefore, an effective public official should encourage open dialogue and facilitate the understanding of cultural groups that interact.

When any individual understands the working language differently, tasks become impaired. The administrator should therefore bear in mind that vocabulary and language style may be a source of many incidents of miscommunication[4]. Likewise, harboring negative perceptions of a cultural group could also be unhealthy because it can lead to disrespectful treatment of others. The challenge is to search for new ways to create understanding of the different interacting value systems as well as improving communication by minimizing the gap of misunderstanding of the interacting cultural systems[5].

Choose the Appropriate Types and Channels of Communication

In most societies, the urgency and importance of a message determines its channel of communication. An effective public administrator should know the channel appropriate for each particular situation. For instance, persons of Arab descent are more likely to recognize the importance of decisions or the urgency of announcements when they receive such face-to-face[5]. Arabs do not encourage discussion on the subject of women; not even the normal Western courtesy of inquiring about the health of wife or daughter. The safe ground is to discuss sports.

Ensure Clarity of Language

When communicating in a multicultural environment, public administrators should ensure that both the spoken and written languages are clear and concise. The advice is not only to be clear but also ensure that verbal as well as nonverbal communications are, reliable, and consistent[7]. Wholesome administrative management requires the same clarity of communication[8].

In negotiations, an Arab would most likely understand the Western direct communication style, whereas the Westerner is unlikely to understand the indirect and implicit style of an Arab. However, by leading the way and making spoken and written language clear and concise, an Arab is likely to do the same.

Avoid Ethnocentrism and Be Sensitive to Cultural Differences

Ethnocentrism occurs when individuals believe that theirs are the only correct values, norms, memes, and beliefs or are the superior ones. Ethnocentrism does not always arise from prejudice, but rather more to inexperience and lack of knowledge of foreign cultures that constitute the cornerstone of international transactions. Public officials serving abroad should recognize the existence of cultural differences between parent and host countries and learn to accept and understand those differences. These administrators should therefore develop the knowledge and working understanding of the cultural context in which the communication takes place[9] and also accept that it may be necessary to change habits or mind-sets when communicating across culture[10].

In most Arab countries, women are excluded from certain environments, are separated from men at public places, are not expected to go out in the company of males who are not their husband or relatives, and are not allowed to drive. Religious leaders justify the ban on women driving cars on the grounds that "the unsupervised movement of individual women whenever and wherever they want to go encourages sexual misconduct[11]. As Carol Frausto, a single woman and the first female commercial officer at the United States Embassy in Riyadh, Saudi Arabia, explains, because wives are often excluded from social gatherings or entertained separately, she was often the only woman at official business functions[12]. A typical ethnocentric behavior might include disdain for this kind of treatment of women due to a lack of understanding of the religious and cultural underpinnings of the gender-bias in male-female relationships in Saudi Arabia. The issue of ethnocentrism can effectively be addressed through cultural sensitivity trainings.

Recognize and Deal with Miscommunication Problems Promptly

Problems emanating from cultural misconceptions and miscommunications in multicultural workplaces are often subtle. The public administrator constantly needs to be on the lookout for the telltale signs of such problems. Miscommunications in multicultural workplaces often go unnoticed, are simply ignored, or are blamed on character flaws of the communicator[13]. Public administrators should stay in tune with the way interpersonal relationships develop and should recognize simmering problems and step in before full-blown conflicts erupt. This skill is also important when negotiating because it gives one the ability to recognize some emotional signs that usually influence the outcomes of negotiation.

Develop Prenegotiation Relationships

Cultural undertones exist in the understanding and perception of the purpose of negotiations. From the perspective of the American society, the purpose of negotiations is essentially to arrive at and sign a binding contract. In the Asian, Arab, Chinese, and Japanese cultures, however, the major essence of negotiation is not a signed contract, but rather the creation of a relationship[14]. The purpose of prenegotiation activities in these cultures is to establish trust. Essentially, negotiations in an international setting are about trust and mutual respect, so the orientation should focus toward long-term commitments rather than toward making a deal[15]. Personal relationships and interactions usually have positive impacts on cross-cultural negotiations. For example, in negotiations, Arabs seek to build rapport with bargaining partners and commence serious negotiations only after initiating personalized relationships through face-to-face meetings[16]. Managers are advised to stay in tune with the way interpersonal relationships develop and to recognize simmering problems and step in before full-blown conflicts erupt[17]. This skill is important when negotiating. It gives one the ability to pick some emotional signs that usually influence the outcomes of negotiation. Another advice is to look for cues regarding whether people are pleased or angry and then amplify their importance[18].

Avoid Stereotyping (Understand That Subcultures Exist)

Stereotyping arises when the assumption is made that all people within one culture or group behave, believe, feel, and act in the same way. A good number of cultures, however, have subcultures. One culture cannot therefore be a stereotype of the entire group because not everyone in a culture has exactly the same values. Moreover, the cultural dynamics within most cultures are complex and are made up of different religious and ethnic groups. Citizens from countries with great cultural diversity often exhibit strong ethnic affinities to their group, and misidentifying them could bring some unexpected measures of animosity. Generalizations can be dangerous because in many ways there are greater differences within any given culture than between one culture and another[19]. Making quick assumptions about the cultural groups of colleagues or negotiation counterparts may undermine other meaningful efforts. For instance, the culture of the Ibos of largely Christian southern Nigeria is quite different and distinct from the culture of the mainly Muslim north. Similarly, there is no homogeneity in the values, beliefs, and behavior patterns in the so-called "Asian culture"[20]. One should therefore not jump to conclusions based on limited knowledge; when in doubt, seek clarifications[21].

Build Trust and Good Relationships

Another way to be an effective public administrator when serving abroad is to develop a rapport built on understanding, especially when involved in team tasks[22]. The key to this is, showing the willingness to listen to others. For effective cross-cultural communication, public administrators need to develop cultural sensitivity[23]. Moreover, outcomes are positive when public administrators show open-mindedness, respect, and patience when dealing across cultures[24]. Mistrust sometimes constitutes a barrier to mutual respect, and whenever it arises it must be overcome by creating trust and credibility. Personal relationships and interactions usually have positive impacts on cross-cultural negotiations in some societies. In negotiating in Saudi Arabia, personal relationships, trust and confidence are very important. Essentially, Arabs seek to build a long-term relationship with their bargaining partner[25].

Acquire Knowledge of the Hosts' Language and Mode of Communication

An acquisition of a rudimentary knowledge of certain aspects of a host's language and modes of communication is necessary and leads to better communication. Learning the basic language for greeting others and shopping (even when associates speak English) is quite important[26]. An obvious or implied disrespectfulness for the hosts' modes of communications should be avoided. For instance, the Arabs show bonding and friendship through such gestures as same-sex cheek kissing and hugging. In the same way, a same-sex arm link is a nonverbal indicator of trust, friendship, and bonding. Friendly arm linking between two males in Arab, African, and Latin American cultures is a commonplace practice[27]. This, in some Western cultures, may be incorrectly interpreted as an indication of sexual orientation, and an outward show of disapproval or discomfort could cause unexpected problems. Foreign serving administrators should therefore be open-minded about accepting the new culture and avoid overt or implied criticisms of local practices and customs[28].

Know the Do's and Don'ts of communication in host country

Business communication in an interpersonal environment is a people-oriented behavior; to accomplish their responsibilities, without any major complications, international business executives will have to observe the rules of conduct of the host country in which they are doing business[29]. These rules determine the appropriate modes of communication that indicate what to do and what not to do. This could apply to negotiation too. For instance, the Saudis attach a great deal of importance to status; it is therefore, not so beneficial to send junior managers to business meetings with senior Saudi executives who would surely feel slighted by such. Also, on a negotiating table one does not pointedly disagree with the Saudis as disagreeing with a Saudi in the presence of others is an impoliteness in the Arab world and may be difficult to remedy[30]. The Saudis also do not like male acquaintances asking after their daughters or wives.

Granted, cross-cultural communication inherent in multi-cultural organizations presents a myriad of problems, there are obvious advantages there from diversifying the workplaces. Such advantages include the fact that culturally diverse workplaces can enhance creativity, lead to better decision-making processes and result into effectiveness and productivity. A mono-cultural workplace does not enjoy the benefit of diverse opinions, multi-talented worker pool and multiple propensities for creativity. Cultural diversity also prevents 'one-way' thinking (group think) where group members are culturally pressurized to agree with mainstream thinking for fear of been characterized as saboteurs or as ignoramuses. The major trend in today's business is that companies are now accepting the fact that these differences enable them to compete globally and acquire rich sources of new talents.

Chapter 13
Organizational Strategies for Developing Global Management Skills

Foreign assignments are important mechanism for developing the international expertise of both employees and the organization. The level of support an organization offers its expatriate or foreign-serving employees sometimes affect the outcome of the posting. Some these employees or officers even return simply because they are not happy with their assignments due to poor organizational support by the home office[1]. There are needs for management support especially because, the ultimate goal of strategic human resources should be "to support, manage and maintain high-commitment and high-performance employees"[2]. Such on-the-job supports could come in form of assistance with children's education, being in constant communication with the expatriates, and trouble shooting.

The need for an effective and competent expatriation has remained as dire as ever. This becomes more imperative when one considers the fact that "the real cost of an unsuccessful international expatriate extends beyond the monetary expenses of compensation. An unsuccessful expatriate almost invariably has a negative impact on the future interactions between the multinational companies and their host countries[3]. To achieve this new expatriation measures have to be added to the existing ones. One recommends that the company adopts the following measures.

The purpose of every training exercise is to increase the probability of attaining set goals. Training is therefore of particular importance to oversea assignments because it enhances the possibilities for tapping the full potentials of the concerned officer[4]. Training helps the officers serving abroad understand the customs and cultures of the host countries. The topics usually covered in this cultural training are customs, social and cultural etiquette, history, politics, local suspicions, and local rivalries[5]. An effective and competent global management skill becomes an imperative when one considers that the cost of an unsuccessful international assignment extends beyond the monetary expenses. An unsuccessful foreign assignment could have a negative impact on future interactions or hurt nation-to-nation relationships[6]. The challenge is to search for new ways to understand the different value systems involved and reinforced through traditions, as well as ways to minimize the gap between the cultural differences and to improve effective communication in international business[7]. The following proactive measures that are supported by experts' opinion are hereby recommended. They include; use of cultural assimilators, cultural integrators, workplace diversification, and in-house sensitivity.

Cultural Assimilators

Cultural assimilators are learning techniques, programmed to show the basic norms, customs, attitudes, and values of various countries. This cultural assimilator model has become one of the most effective approaches toward improvement in cross-cultural competence[8]. Exposing a public administrator preparing to serve abroad to some basic cultural sensitivity training could be done through this assimilation program. Most of the cultural assimilators essentially require the trainee to read or observe puzzling incidents or interactions, and interpret the situation. Cultural assimilators assist in the reduction of the novelty of the host cultures, thereby reducing the potential cultural shocks associated with new foreign assignments.

From the onset, it is necessary to expose employees to diversity even when such employees still reside in the parent country. One way to do this could be subject employees, as Adler suggested, to working in multicultural groups where team members have diverse cultural backgrounds[9]. Another way would be the development of cultural assimilators for the countries the company operates in. Cultural assimilators are programmed learning techniques that would show the basic norms, customs, attitudes and values of the various countries. The programs are usually designed to foster an appreciation of the local culture so that the expatriate can develop appropriate coping patterns. In Arab cultures, for instance, emphasis is placed on personal relationship, trust and respect in business dealing, with religion permeating every aspect of life. The cultural assimilators would likely assist in the reduction of the novelty of those cultures to the employees.

Cultural Integrators

This model involves placing individuals who are vastly knowledgeable in the local cultures in each foreign program, operation, or location. This is the model sometimes deployed by the United States military in Afghanistan as it embeds the locals into its operations, campaigns, and rebuilding efforts. These integrators advise and guide the actions needed to ensure smooth and synchronized operations[10]. The primary purpose of this model is to improve the effectiveness of interactions with local personnel and citizens.

Workplace Diversification

Organizations and departments that have special interests or commitments in particular countries could use workplace recruitment of individuals from those cultures as means of enhancing cultural competence. From the outset, it is necessary to expose employees to diversity even when such officers still reside in the home country. A way to do this is to make the officers work in multicultural groups in which team members have diverse cultural backgrounds[11]. Spy agencies, nations at war, international development agencies, and law enforcement agencies use this model.

In-House Cultural Sensitivity Training

The essence of in-house competence training is to sensitize the workers about the cultures of the host countries. This is necessary because creating cultural competence in multicultural environments requires education and training[12]. The development of cultural competence through multicultural interactions in the workplace gives a better appreciation of foreign assignment experiences and skills[13]. This competence training includes not only the ability to apply language skills to situations but also the ability to make good use of communication to attain organizational goals[14]. This involves exposing the officers to the culture and values of the host country. These vast cultural peculiarities could include food, manner of speech, acceptable noise levels, gender, and religious issues.

To hasten adaptability of officers working abroad, this in-house cultural training starts in the home country and should be continued in the host country. In addition, this training should be offered to the officer's family members because a foreign assignment is more likely to succeed if the spouse and children continue to have a positive perception of the posting.

Cross-Cultural Competence Models

Organizations could use cross cultural communication models to develop, enhance, and assess the global competence levels of managers. The cross cultural communication competence model (3C model) developed by Alexei Matveev, Nagesh Rao, and Richard

Milter in 2001 identified four dimensions: (i) interpersonal skills, (ii) team effectiveness, (iii) cultural uncertainty, and (iv) cultural empathy[15]. Readers are hereby, referred to appendix A on page 111.

Interpersonal skills entail that a team member acknowledges communicative and interactional differences between the cultures, shows flexibility in resolving misunderstanding and miscommunications, and fells comfortable when communication people from other cultures. Team effectiveness is the ability of team member to understand and clearly communicate team goals, roles, and procedures to other members of the multicultural team. The cultural uncertainty is the ability to display patience in intercultural situations, and be tolerant of ambiguities and uncertainties that arise from cultural differences. Cultural empathy is to ability to behave as though one understands the world as other team members from other cultures do, has inquisitiveness of other cultures, appreciate differences in working styles, and non-ethnocentrisms. These cross cultural communication competence dimensions are learned behaviors that can be enhanced through training[16].

To function effectively and achieve high levels of team performance, the global manager must possess effective cross cultural communication competence[17]. Effective global managers will not only recognize the approaches of other cultures towards work and decision-making, but will also adapt communications to accommodate his or her knowledge of the other cultures[18].

Continuous Expatriate training

To hasten adaptability of the expatriate employees, the expatriate (cultural) training that starts in the home country should be continued in the host country. The training process should be designed to alter the employee's attitudes and behavior in such a manner as to increase the probability of attaining the organizational goals. This involves exposing the employee to the culture and values of the host country, enable the manager better understand the customs and work habits of the local culture. . These vast cultural peculiarities would include food, manner of speech, acceptable noise levels, gender, and religion issues. One way to do this would to embed a cultural integrator, who would advise, guide and recommend actions and would ensure better understanding of the local culture. This should also be offered to the family because an expatriate assignment is more likely to be successful if the spouse continues to have a positive perception of the posting.

Chapter 14
Cultural Competences for the Global Manager

Most of the problems encountered during intercultural business, governmental or international interactions arise from the lack of understanding of the basic cultural differences among the countries of the world. To conduct interactions across cultures, the global manager or foreign-serving officer must be willing to make efforts to understand and work within the cultural context of the foreign country. This is because, with the increasingly multinational relationships of today, it is critical that officials serving abroad not only have the necessary technical expertise but also possess cultural knowledge of host countries. Hence, sound management of officials in foreign assignments is of critical importance for creating and maintaining good relationships with collaborating and negotiating partners. To achieve success in foreign assignments, it is therefore important to surpass cultural differences and ethnocentrism, and promote interaction between cultures.

Choosing and training the managers to send abroad for international assignments are usually difficult and expensive for both the manager and the organization. The stress of an unfamiliar environment and the subsequent cultural shock even makes is difficult for the manager to perform effectively. Being able to communicate effectively across cultural differences, understanding how to navigate complex sociocultural situations, and being familiar with the customs and norms of many cultures are important skills for global management. Employees who are able to develop close relationships with people from different cultural, racial or economic background are likely to acculturate more easily in foreign duties.

The need, therefore, exists to exercise care and adopt the appropriate criteria in choosing the managers who are most likely to meet the challenges of working in unfamiliar environments and cultures. Apart from the obvious technical and managerial abilities, cultural-oriented criteria for choosing the global manager would include cultural empathy, cross-cultural communication competence, adaptability, and having global perspectives.

Global Perspectives

This is the capacity to broaden one's focus from local or two-country perspective to a global perspective. This creates the ability to compare and evaluate the requirement parameters as one deal with issues in alien cultural environments. Essentially, the global manager can cope with situations and people who are different from his or her background and is willing to re-examine and alter personal attitudes and perspectives. A good global manager is, therefore, capable of operating effectively in a global environment while being respectful of cultural diversity.

Cultural responsiveness

This refers to the ability to take one's culture and fuse it into another culture, thereby making the resulting cultural orientation unique one. To achieve this calls for diverse ways of thinking and respect for other people's culture. This capacity allows the global manager to unify varying perspectives of different societal and organizational cultures, thereby avoiding counterproductive ethno-centric biases. The global manager is required to be familiar with other cultures. Thinking globally and at same time responding locally.

Appreciation of Cultural Synergies

Cultural synergy is the cooperative action that can occur when diverse groups of people with varying cultural orientation work together. The objective is to increase effectiveness by sharing unique perceptions, values and insights towards the mutual achievement of set goals. This, however, calls for learning and understanding the dynamics of multicultural situations. When there is synergy in a multicultural work environment, something new is born, and "the whole becomes greater than the sum of the parts". Under a condition of cultural synergy, the sub-cultures working together are more likely to accomplish more than those same units working separately. The benefit of cultural synergy therefore rests on the belief that when solving problems, groups are smarter than the people within. The global manager uses the cultural synergy that is built through collaboration that integrates the cultural difference to enrich both the human and organizational activities[1]. This means the ability to build upon the differences in culture for mutual growth and accomplishment through cooperation[2]. The recognition by the global manger of the potential for cultural synergy leads to the appreciation of the need for adaptability. This recognition of the beneficial outcomes of cultural synergy leads to better cross-cultural understanding and respect for cultural sensitivities.

Cultural Adaptability

Cultural adaptability is the willingness and ability to recognize, understand and work effectively across cultural differences. For the global manager, adapting to the culture in which she or he lives or conducts business is a desired capability. The global manager is required to develop the ability to live and work effectively in many different cultures. The global manager requires the capacity for cultural adaptability because the differences in cultural orientation often affect how people interact, work and manage. A global manager who is keen on developing cultural adaptability must understand the foundations of the relevant areas of the foreign culture; and must learn how the foreign culture views important aspects of work and life.

Cross-cultural communication competence

To be a successful global manager, one would have to be a successful cross-cultural communicator. In selecting managers for foreign assignments, an organization should, therefore, take the willingness to communicate in an alien language into consideration. Adjustment would be very difficult if a manager does not know how to communicate rudimentarily in the host country's language. Language proficiency would help the manager communicate with coworkers and that would help him/her learn the appropriate work values, expectations and standards[3]. Proficiency in host's language is, however, not just enough; it is the willingness to communicate that is most important.

Non-Ethnocentrism

Ethnocentrism is the tendency to regard one's group and culture as superior to other groups and cultures[4]. Non-ethnocentricity tendencies constitute another consideration. The non-ethno centrist is likely to have and for easy and faster adjustment .Hence, ethnocentrism is usually treated as a drawback because it has been found to have a negative influence cross-cultural adjustment[5].

Cross-cultural collaboration

The ability to work effectively in multicultural teams is requirement for global management. This ability to focus on positive results or implications of cross-cultural collaboration makes the global manager function effectively in the multicultural environments that which permeates today's business world. The successful global managers are, therefore, those willing and able to understand and work effectively across cultural differences.

Tolerance for Cultural Shocks

The global manager should have adequate tolerance for cultural shocks. This entails the willingly welcoming opportunities to go to different countries to experience culturally different environments. Cultural shock, therefore, need not be a negative experience for the global manager.

Ethical Sensitivity

Ethics are the moral principles or values that govern whether actions are right or wrong, and outcomes good or bad. Decision makers face larger set of ethical dilemmas when they enter the global market[6]. Ethical sensitivity is therefore, that personal characteristic that enables one to recognize the presence, and determine the relative importance of an ethical issue. This enables the global manager estimate the moral intensity of actions and therefore, deals with any ethical issues that may arise.

Chapter 15
Ethical Issues in Global Management

When business is conducted across national and cultural boundaries, ethical issues take on added layers of complexity. Nations operate in multiple regions, each with distinct cultures and subcultures. It is quite common for officers on foreign assignments to be born into a culture distinctively different from the one in which they work or interact. Hence, it is important to understand the ethical values of the different cultures with which they interact. Understanding the ethical values of these different cultures would likely create the required synergies in cross-cultural interactions.

Ethics are a system of moral principles, constituting the moral compass that guides individuals in personal decision making. Ethics are about right and wrong, good and bad, benefit and harm, and they define the nature of public managers and administrators[1]. Ethics, simply put, involve one's rights and duties, the rules one applies in making decisions, and how one's actions affect other people[2]. These standards of conduct indicate how one should behave based on moral duties and virtues that constitute the ethics of the organization or society. Usually an individual has an internal set of standards, values, and principles that guide one's everyday decision making. The challenge in comprehending ethics rests on its subjectivity, its intangibility, and, to some extent, its spirituality.

Culture, which is, the standard that determines the 'rightness' of the individual's behavior in a given society, can have effects on the ethical orientation of the individual[3]. In fact, specific ethical or moral principles are what define a cultural group's identity. Hence, the values considered ethical by one culture may differ from those of another. Whereas some practices are acceptable in some societies, they are not in others; hence cultural differences make ethical decisions more difficult[4].

Ethical issues tend to exist in most public decision-making processes, and ethical dilemmas arise when right or wrong are not clearly identified and each alternative has a potentially harmful ethical consequence. The issues of ethics have acquired more importance in recent times because interactions between governments, organizations, and foreign countries have become more frequent, and primordial interests no longer govern activities and decisions. Other reasons include the increasing scope of domestic legislative enactments and the global concerns about such issues as child labor, pollution, economic exploitation, and workplace safety. Again, understanding the ethical values of different cultures helps create the required synergies in cross-cultural interactions. .

On the international front, however, this difficulty in making ethical decisions is exacerbated by the marked differences in value systems and practices. It therefore becomes incumbent upon the administrator to understand these culture differences when issues of ethics and values arise. Although recent research has begun to shed some light upon these differences, there remains much uncharted territory. From ethical considerations, the global manager must know when to limit accommodations to other cultures and values and when to impose his or her own values on other cultures. The moral approach to global assignments requires managers to be cognizant of the consequences of their actions in terms of their impact on values such as liberty, justice, and human dignity[5].

The goal should be to endeavor to balance the necessity of building and sustaining those personal relationships with the need to maintain the required professional standards. A guideline in doing this is to analyze ethical issues locally while keeping an eye on their global dimensions. Thinking locally and acting globally is a strategic concept that enjoins organizations to respond to local environments and at the same time consider their global implications. These situations sometimes lead to contradictions, but the manager should be able to navigate whatever contradictions might arise. The focus, however, should on preserving and protecting such fundamental core human values as good citizenship, respect for human dignity, respect for basic human rights, and equity. The global manager must, therefore, work for the adoption of adequate workplace and environment health and safety standards, the payment of basic living wages, equal employment opportunity, and refraining from child labor.

Essentially, such issues as bribery, environmental degradation, child labor, human rights abuses, apartheid, and discrimination based on race, gender, and disabilities and a host of other issues have been universally accepted as unethical according to United Nations declarations and should never be compromised. The Caux Roundtable Principles for Business Conduct developed in Caux, Switzerland by European, North America, and Japanese business leaders should serve as a useful guide for global managers[6]. The Caux principles aim at promoting the values of mutual prosperity under healthy and fair completion and human dignity by promoting free trade, environmental and cultural integrity, and the prevention of bribery and corruption.

Chapter 16
Summaries of Business and Work Attitudes of National Clusters

Anglo Countries (United States, Canada, Australia, the United Kingdom, New Zealand, and Ireland)
The personal and business attitudes of Anglo countries are oriented toward personal achievement and performance. The style of communication is direct; messages are direct, concise and explicit. Although individuals will likely express their feeling in a first business contact, reasoning, rather than emotions, dominates one's interactions with business partners. As specific societies, private and business lives are separated.

Individuals in these countries focus on formal rules and expect their business associates to do the same. Legal contracts are, therefore, readily drawn up. Individuals believe the can control what happens to them, and are, therefore, architects of their own fortune. Individuals in these societies also tend do one thing at a time, keep appointments strictly, and follow plans to the letter.

Workers strive for personal achievements, are usually

competitive, and tend to accept personal responsibility for successes as well as failures. They are relatively more tolerant of behaviors and opinions that differ from theirs because they do not feel threatened by them. Respect is accorded based on how well the person has performed or what the person has accomplished. Importance is placed on job, work performance, skills, and education. Subordinates and superiors perceive and treat each other as colleagues who have equal rights. Subordinates expect, therefore, to have inputs in the decisions or actions affecting them.

These cultures also have strong belief in standard operating procedures, value specialization, and respect the opinion of experts. In these societies, workers place more importance on earnings, recognition, advancement, challenge and wealth. Workers in these societies usually experience higher job stress. The leadership styles in such societies are often participatory.

Germanic countries (Switzerland, Germany, and Austria)

These are also, achievement society where rewards and honor come with personal achievement and performance. Styles of communication are also direct. Legal contracts are also readily drawn up.

In these societies, however, individuals will hardly express their feeling in a first business contact and strive to hold their emotions in check. Reasoning, rather than emotions, also dominates one's interactions with business partners. People also do one thing at a time, keep appointments strictly, and follow plans to the letter.

People also believe they can control what happens to them.

Workers also strive for personal achievements while accepting personal responsibility for successes as well as failures. Employees are also relatively more tolerant of behaviors and opinions that differ from theirs. Respect is accorded based on how well the person has performed or what the person has accomplished. Subordinates and superiors perceive and treat each other as colleagues who have equal rights.

Individuals believe, however, that practices can be applied everywhere without modification, tend to focus on formal rules and expect their business associates to do the same. Importance is placed on job, work performance, skills, and education. Focus is more on rules than relationships. Workers are more likely to question their bosses, and participative management is more likely to be used.

Nordic countries (Sweden, Denmark, Norway, Finland, and The Netherlands)

In these societies, people feel awkward at public display of emotions, and will, therefore, hardly express their feeling in a first business contact. Individuals also keep appointments strictly, and follow plans to the letter. Focus is also more on rules than relationships, and legal contracts are readily drawn up.

In these societies, people tend to feel secured, and are relatively more tolerant of behaviors and opinions that differ from their own. Subordinates and superiors also perceive and treat each other as colleagues who have equal rights. Organizations, however, place emphasis on cooperation and team achievement. Workers place great importance on cooperation, employment security, and friendly work environment. The workers are also more likely to question their bosses, and participative management is more likely to be used. Workers in these societies tend to experience less work stress.

Near East Countries (Greece, Iran, Yugoslavia, and Turkey)

Individuals tend to focus on relationships; working things out to suit their business partners. Business opportunities revolve around the government and its agencies; and are mostly dispensed through personal relationships. These official transactions are, however, often friendship-based; and can therefore, be said to be conducted only after trust has been well established. Relationships are in multiple spheres that involve both official and private lives.

Employees tend to work in teams and accept responsibility jointly. Workers are reluctant to accept the pay-for-performance system of the Anglo-Saxon societies. Superiors are expected to lead and make decisions. Employment, organizational ascendancy, and organizational transactions are usually done on basis of personal relationship. Bonds of friendship and relationship are usually stronger than rules; and individuals are more likely to exhibit a higher degree of nepotism or favoritism in such matters as employment and contract awards. Employees are more likely to obey the orders of their superiors and are less likely to question authority. The leadership styles in such societies are predominantly autocratic or paternalistic.

Arabic Countries (Saudi Arabia, United Arab Emirates, Bahrain, Kuwait, Oman, Abu-Dhabi, Bahrain, Egypt, Iraq, Kuwait, Lebanon, Libya, Oman, Saudi Arabia, United Arab Emirates)

Individuals in these cultures also usually conduct business only after trust has been well established. They also tend to focus on relationships; working things out to suit their business partners. Relationships play visible roles in all aspects of life; and most official and businesses are transacted on that basis. Business opportunities revolve around the government and its agencies; and are most times, are developed and dispensed through personal relationships. Relationships are also in multiple spheres that involve official and private lives. People express their emotions openly. Individuals tend do more than one thing at a time, and appointments are approximate. People allure outcomes more to predestination than to personal efforts.

Employees also tend to work in teams and accept responsibility jointly, and have long-term commitment to groups and common interests. Workers condone high level of inequality of power and wealth and are, therefore, more likely to condone hierarchical organizational systems. Employees are also more likely to obey the orders of their superiors and are less likely to question authority; and also lean toward believing that circumstances should dictate how practices should be applied.

The bonds of friendship and relationship in these

societies are usually stronger than rules; and individuals are more likely to exhibit a higher degree of nepotism or favoritism in such matters as employment and contract awards. Employment, organizational ascendancy, and organizational transactions are usually on basis of personal relationship.

Far East Countries (Philippines, Hong Kong, Malaysia, Singapore, Taiwan, Indonesia, South Vietnam, and Thailand).

Individuals in these societies also tend to focus on relationships. People in these societies will hardly express their feeling in a first business contact, feel awkward at public display of emotions, and could show displeasure with physical contact outside private life. Reasoning, rather than emotions, dominates one's interactions with business partners. Here also, economic opportunities revolve more around the government and its agencies; and are most times, dispensed are developed through personal relationships. These relationships are also in multiple spheres that involve official and private lives, and individuals tend do more than one thing at a time, thereby making appointments very much approximate.

Employees not only tend to achieve and accept responsibility jointly, but also accept high level of inequality of power and wealth. Superiors are expected to lead, to make decisions autocratically and paternalistically, and subordinates are generally afraid and unwilling to disagree with their superiors. Although workers relatively more tolerant of differing behaviors and opinions, they believe that circumstances should dictate how practices should be applied. Bonds of friendship and relationship are usually stronger than rules and individuals are, therefore, more likely to exhibit a higher degree of nepotism or favoritism.

From the Confucian long-term orientation, organizations are more likely to emphasize education, training, thriftiness and delay of immediate gratification. Individuals in these societies are, however, more likely to allude to fate as an explanation for personal outcomes; and are, therefore, less likely than the Western cultures to be upset when a business deals fails to go through.

Latin America ((Argentina, Venezuela, Chile, Mexico, Peru, and Colombia)

Workers in these societies tend to achieve jointly as well as assume joint responsibility. The employees are comfortable with high level of inequality of power and wealth and are therefore, more likely to obey the orders of their superiors and are less likely to question authority. The workers tend to accept the perspective that circumstances should dictate how practices should be applied. Bonds of friendship and relationship are usually stronger than rules; and individuals are more likely to exhibit a higher degree of nepotism or favoritism in such matters as employment and contract awards. Employment, organizational ascendancy, and organizational transactions are usually done on basis of personal relationship.

Latin European (France, Belgium, Italy, Spain, and Portugal)

These societies focus is more on relationship than rules; and legal contracts are readily modified. The individuals do not hesitate to show their emotions, either verbally or nonverbally. In these diffused societies also, one's official life also permeates the private and every other area of life. Interpersonal relationships are all encompassing involving official, private and every other facet of life. One's official titles are also used in private settings.

Employees not only accept high level of inequality of power and wealth but also believe that circumstances should dictate how practices should be applied. Bonds of friendship and relationship are usually stronger than rules. Organizations in these societies have hierarchical structures and employees are comfortable with higher centralization of decision making process than the Germanic and Anglo countries.

Sub-Saharan African (Nigeria, Ghana, Kenya, Ethiopia, Zambia and Sierra Leone)

In these societies, even official interactions are friendship-based and more often; official assistances are rendered on the basis of personal relationship. Business opportunities revolve around the government and its agencies; and are most times, are developed and dispensed through personal relationships. Relationships are in multiple spheres that involve official and private lives with the individuals doing more than one thing at a time; thereby making appointment times what approximate.

The workers are comfortable with high power distance that indicates high level of inequality in power and wealth; and status and respect are accorded based on who or what the person is; and importance is placed as age, gender, family, ethnic group

Workers tend toward the belief that circumstances should dictate how practices should be applied. The bonds of friendship and relationship are usually stronger than rules; and individuals are therefore, more likely to exhibit a higher degree of nepotism or favoritism in such matters as employment and contract awards.

The employees in organizations in these countries are more likely to obey the orders of their superiors and are less likely to question authority. Moreover, superiors are expected to lead, to make decisions autocratically and paternalistically, and subordinates are generally afraid and unwilling to disagree with their superiors. Employment, organizational ascendancy, and organizational transactions are, therefore, usually done on basis of personal relationship and power structure.

Chapter 17
Snapshots of Work and Organizational Attitudes in Some Nations

CHINA

In China, strong social ties exist among societal members, with each member primarily concerned with the prevailing interest of the in-group, thereby tending towards sharing similar beliefs, and feelings of harmonious interdependence. The Chinese culture emphasizes social duty and the impacts of one's actions on others. People mostly derive their identities from one's connection to in-groups such as family, clan, or employer; and the concerns for entities larger than oneself foster an appreciation for cooperation, harmony, conformity, and loyalty. Peoples with this cultural orientation usually regard family harmony and relationships as the foundation on which societies are organized, and, therefore stress family and kinship relations when doing business. The Chinese also place high value on family/referent group which is further enhanced by the socialistic influence of communism.

The Chinese cultural tradition is founded on the

Confucian value that emphasizes hierarchy, contending that each individual should be conscious of his or her position in the social system and is, therefore, is renowned for being authority oriented. The people of China are, therefore, characterized by long-term orientation they had derived from the ethos of Confucianism. This culture is then more likely to emphasize education, training, thriftiness and delay of immediate gratification. In business dealings, the Chinese are more likely to prefer long-term rather than short-term relationships.

The large power distance and weak uncertainty avoidance of the Chinese leads to the view of the organization as an extended family, with managers and organizational heads are considered parent figures but with few formal rules. Organizations in China are, therefore, likely to be hierarchical, with the managers exhibiting the propensity toward autocratic leadership. Subordinates do not participate in the decision-making process. The subordinates, however, have the ability to participate indirectly by influencing the leader or other participants who are expectedly also members of the in-group.

The Chinese cultural type is usually highly concerned with uncertainty avoidance and hence places emphasis on formalization and standardization, giving little allowance for innovative behaviors from managers. Organizational managers prefer team-based work groups with strong control by supervisors. In organizational leadership, the Chinese might prefer autocratic styles with the subordinates offering their loyalty and obedience. A leadership that adopts an autocratic style may be more accepted and effective in a high power distance culture as China than the western world. Although with wealth increasingly becoming part of the Chinese value system and some key elements of the culture are undergoing changes; the respects for authority and collectivist orientation remain unchanged.

Organizations in China are more likely to emphasize security of job tenure, appreciate experts and their knowledge, and have more written rules and procedures, less risk taking by managers. These organizations tend to have bureaucratic rules and are usually hierarchical; trusting only family and friend to handles important assignment. Managers are less likely to share information with subordinates, who are also most unlikely to participate in decision making. Organizations in China accept such outward show of power as protocol, chain command, and respect for existing hierarchy. In these organizations, rewards and redress of grievances are usually at the direction of the power holders, rather than corporate procedures. Essentially, the societal systems operate with a collective aggressive and achievement-driven organizational and supervisory style.

Unlike the Americans who consider the goal of negotiation as a signed contract, the Chinese often consider the goal of negotiation, as the creation of relationship. For Americans, signing a contract is closing a deal; for the Chinese, it is the opening of a relationship. In negotiations, the Chinese prefer the general principles; any unexpected circumstances will be dealt with on the basis of an existing relationship and on the basis of a contract. The Chinese stress team negotiations and consensus decision-making, which takes more time to negotiate a deal.

The Confucian undertone of the East Asian culture proposes moderation and avoidance of acts or tactics that are capable of destroying harmony. The need to build relationships and harmony, therefore, also influences the negotiation tactics of business organizations in China. This East Asian culture is, however, more likely to allude to fate as an explanation for personal outcomes. They are, therefore, less likely than the western cultures to be upset when a business deal fails to come through.

UNITED STATES

In the United States, individuals look after their own self-interests or the interest of small groups to which they have ties, such as the immediate family. Generally, individuals in this society, therefore, value autonomy, competition, self-determination, and pursuit of self-interest. As an achievement society, rewards and honor come with personal achievement and performance; and not much importance is attached to status and rank. The needs for personal recognition, therefore, tend to foster an appreciation for competition. Employees, therefore, crave the feelings of personal accomplishment and individual recognition for a job well done and for efforts that exceed those of others. Note that members of the United States armed forces are usually given congressional honors only when they act "above and beyond the call of duty."

Organizations in the United States appreciate experts and their knowledge, and have some written rules and procedures, tend to encourage moderate risk taking by managers. In this society, organizations have more ambitious employees, and higher employee turn-over. United States business organizations avoid hierarchy; considering such as inefficient and counterproductive. They also tend to value competence over seniority. The organizational systems operate with an aggressive and individual achievement-driven organizational and supervisory style.

The organizational designs in the United States usually emphasizes horizontal relationships, are relatively decentralized, and low in specialization and formalization. Formalization will be characterized by such things as organizational charts, information booklets, operating instructions, and written job descriptions, procedure manuals, written policies, and work-flow schedules and programs. This organizational design entails that workers be given particular functions and expected to stay in that area and develop functional expertise. The management systems are, therefore, decentralized system and decision-making pushed down the line so as to get the lower-level personnel involved.

The organization is perceived as an institution with dynamic, entrepreneurial, risk taking and innovative culture; with no decisive hierarchy, flexible rules and problem solving orientation. Although the initiative belongs to the organizational leaders, subordinates are usually allowed to participate in the decision making process.

Managers in the United States are, therefore, more likely to share information with subordinates, and conduct less autocratic leadership style that encourages participative decision-making. Decision-making in in most American organizations is basically carried out by the individual departmental head or manager, with responsibility usually assigned to individuals. There is a general preference for egalitarian and consultative management practices; and managers are expected to maintain perception of equality with subordinates. Managers, therefore, place less emphasis on formalization; with the organizations adopting smaller power distance between managers and subordinates. Organizations also create job-based work designs that hinge on individual initiative and responsibility.

In negotiations, Americans tend to follow the approach of using a leader who has complete authority to take decisions during the proceedings. This moderate risk avoidance country usually has few people in negotiation teams, and can act quickly. For Americans, the outcome of a negotiation is a contract/agreement; and signing a contract means closing a deal. The American, therefore, prefers detailed contracts that aim to anticipate all possible circumstances and eventualities.

BRAZIL

Brazil is a moderate individualism cultural type in which some measure of individualism exists with the strong social ties that characterize collectivist societies. Although most people drive their identities from one's connection to in-groups such as family, clan, or employer, some good measure of competitiveness exists. Business relationships do tend to hinge on long-term commitment; and building trust is essentially important for international business dealings. Individuals in this culture are less time-driven are, therefore, less likely to keep to agreed time. In Brazil, authority is vested in higher levels in the organizations and an authority. As a result of influences from the western countries, organizational management has imbibed more formalized rules and procedures. The large power distance and strong uncertainty avoidance of the Brazilian society leads, however, to the perception of the organization as a "pyramid of people" that should have a hierarchical bureaucratic structure. This creates the hierarchical structure of the organization that is held together by the unity of command and rules.

This high risk avoidance society tends to lead to lots of bureaucratic rules, rely on standards and formulas, and trust in only family and friends. These high uncertainty avoidance societies try to socialize the people into trying to beat the unpredictable future by means of laws and expertise. As in most collectivist societies, subordinates do not usually participate; rather the expectation is that the leader leads autocratically without inputs from the subordinates who are simply obey orders and instructions.

Organizations in Brazil are more likely to emphasize security of job tenure, appreciate experts and their knowledge, and have some written rules and procedures, moderate taking by managers. These organizations accept outward show of power as protocol, chain command, and respect for existing hierarchy. Rewards and redress of grievances are usually at the direction of the power holders, rather than corporate procedures.

SAUDI ARABIA

The Saudi society is a collectivist cultural type in which strong social ties exists among societal members; with each member primarily concerned with the prevailing interest of the in-group. Organizations in Saudi Arabia usually prefer autocratic managers who are usually reluctant to trust subordinates. The society emphasizes social duty and concerns for entities larger than oneself, which fosters an appreciation for cooperation, harmony, conformity, and loyalty. Saudi Arabia is a collectivist and high power distant society in which much respect is shown for authorities, titles, birth, and religious status. The society, therefore, makes a distinction between people with status and power and people without it.

In this high uncertainty avoidance society, there is usually higher anxiety, leading to nervousness as society tries to socialize the people into trying to beat the unpredictable future. The society, therefore, tries to create security and avoid risk by using such instruments as laws or religion to protect the society from the unpredictability of human behaviors. The extensive use laws, rules, regulations, and controls are, however, not often for the protection of the rights and interest of the citizens, but rather to reduce the amount of uncertainty in the society. The proliferation of laws also implies intolerance for deviant behaviors and opinions.

Alternatively, they use religion use to make the uncertainty tolerable because religions contain teachings that they believe are beyond uncertainty. As in some high uncertainty societies, there is always one religion that claims absolute truth and thereby showing little tolerance for other religions. The Saudi society also condones the inequalities of wealth and power within them. The Saudis are, therefore, more likely to condone hierarchical systems that do not encourage significant upward mobility of its citizens.

Organizational leadership is highly authoritarian with rigid instructions that reflect the high power distance and high uncertainty avoidance of the society. The organizational structure is highly bureaucratic and over centralized, with authority vested on the top management. Planning is not long-term but is rather ad hoc; and decisions are made at the top echelons of management. Organizations lack vigorous performance evaluation but rather use informal control mechanism with routine checks on performance. Personnel policies include heavy reliance on personal contacts for employment and advancement.

Communication in this society involves a great deal of nonverbal clues; and is further enhanced when interpersonal trust exists. Subordinates do not usually participate in decision-making; rather the expectation is that the leader leads autocratically without inputs from the subordinates who are simply obey orders and instructions. There is, therefore, very little participative leadership. As a collectivist society, however, subordinates could indirectly participate by influencing the leader or other participants who are expectedly also members the in-group.

Organizations in Saudi Arabia are more likely to emphasize security of job tenure, have more written rules and procedures, and less risk taking by managers. These organizations tend to have bureaucratic rules and are usually hierarchical; trusting only family and friend to handles important assignment. Paternalism is a very common leadership style; a boss is would usually be involved in subordinates' marriage, children's welfare and graduation, and bereavements. Organizations also accept outward show of power as protocol, chain command, and respect for existing hierarchy. In these organizations, rewards and redress of grievances are also usually at the direction of the power holders, rather than corporate procedures.

INDIA

India is a collectivist cultural type in which, strong social ties exist among societal members, with each member primarily concerned with the prevailing interest of the in-group. People mostly derive their identities from one's connection to in-groups such as family, clan, or employer. Also, the concerns for entities larger than oneself foster an appreciation for cooperation, harmony, conformity, and loyalty. Emphasis is placed on group orientation; and there is toleration for social castes system and high level of bureaucracy.

The large power distance and weak uncertainty avoidance of India leads to the view of the organization as an extended family with the clan and employee focused orientation. In India, subordinates do not also participate. The expectation also, is that the leader leads autocratically without inputs from the subordinates who are simply obey orders and instructions. As a collectivist society, subordinates can also indirectly participate by influencing the leader or other participants who are expectedly also members the in-group.

The managers and organizational heads are considered parent figures but with few formal rules. Like in Saudi Arabia, organizations in India also accept outward show of power as protocol, chain command, and respect for existing hierarchy. Rewards and redress of grievances are usually at the direction of the power holders, rather than corporate procedures.

APPENDIX A:

Summaries of Cross Cultural Communication Competence (3C) models

Interpersonal Skills	<ul><li>Ability to acknowledge differences in interaction styles</li><li>Ability to deal with misunderstandings</li><li>Comfort when communication with foreign nationals</li><li>Awareness of your cultural conditioning</li><li>Basic knowledge about the country, the culture, and the language of team members</li></ul>
Team Effectiveness	<ul><li>Ability to understand and define team goals, roles and norms</li><li>Ability to give and receive constructive feedback</li><li>Ability to discuss and solve problems</li><li>Ability to deal with conflicts</li><li>Ability to display respect for other team members</li><li>Participatory leadership style</li><li>Ability to work cooperatively</li></ul>

Cultural Uncertainty	<ul><li>Ability to deal with cultural uncertainty</li><li>Ability to display patience</li><li>Tolerance of ambiguity/uncertainty due to cultural differences</li><li>Openness to cultural differences</li><li>Willingness to accept change/risk</li><li>Ability to exercise flexibility</li></ul>
Cultural empathy	<ul><li>Ability to see and understand issues from other's cultural perspective</li><li>Exhibiting a spirit of inquiry about other cultures, values, and beliefs.</li><li>Ability to appreciate dissimilar working styles</li><li>Ability to accept different ways of doing things.</li><li>Non-judgmental on the ways things are done in other cultures</li></ul>

Source: Matveev, Rao, and Milter (2001).

ENDNOTES

CHAPTER 1

[1]Kreitner, Robert and Angelo Kinicki. 2004.
Organizational Behavior. New York: The McGraw-Hill Companies.

[2]Hofstede, Geert. 1983. The cultural relativity of organizational practices and theories. *Journal of International Business Studies* 14(2): 75–89.

[3]Hofstede, Geert. 1980. Culture's Consequences: International differences in work-related values. Beverly Hills: Sage.

[4]Ibid.

[5]Ibid.

[6]Drake, E. Laura. 2001. The Culture-Negotiation Link: Integrative and Distributive Bargaining through a Intercultural Communication Lens, Human Communication Research, 27 (3), 317-338.

[7]Hofstede, Geert. 1983. The cultural relativity of organizational practices and theories.*Journal of International Business Studies* 14(2): 75–89.

[8]Drake, Laura. 2001. The Culture-Negotiation Link: Integrative and Distributive Bargaining through a Intercultural Communication Lens, Human Communication Research, 27 (3), 317-338.

[9]Ibid.

[10]Javidan, Mansour and Robert J. House. 2001. Cultural Acumen for the Global manager: Lessons from GLOBE project. *Organizational Dynamics*, 29(4), 289-305.

[11]Garibaldi de Hilal, Adriana Victoria. 2006. Brazilian National Culture, Organizational Culture and Cultural Agreement. *International journal of Cross Cultural Management.* 6 (2), 139-167.

[12]Griffith, David, Michael Hu and John Ryans, Jr, (2000). Process Standardization across intra- and inter-cultural relationships. Journal of International Business Studies, 31(2), 303-325.

[13]Ibid.

[14]Drake, Laura. 2001. The Culture-Negotiation Link: Integrative and Distributive Bargaining through a Intercultural Communication Lens, Human Communication Research, 27 (3), 317-338.

[15]Ibid.

[16]Ibid.

[17]Hofstede, Geert. 1983. The cultural relativity of organizational practices and theories. *Journal of International Business Studies* 14(2): 75–89.

[18]Lewicki, Roy J., Bruce Barry, and David M. Saunders. 2009. *Negotiations: Readings, Exercises and Cases*. 6th Ed. New York: McGraw-Hill.

[19]Garibaldi de Hilal, Adriana Victoria. 2006. Brazilian National Culture, Organizational Culture and Cultural Agreement. *International journal of Cross Cultural Management.* 6 (2), 139-167.

[20]Triandis, C. Harry. 2004. The Many Dimensions of Culture. *Academy of Management Executive.*Vol.18 (1) pp.88-93.

[21]Kemmelmeier, Markus; Eugene Burnstein; Krum Krunov; Petia Genkova; Chie Kanagara, Mathew Hirshberg; Hans-Peter Erb; Grazyna Wieczorkowska, and Kimberly Noels. 2003. Individualism, collectivism, and authoritarianism in seven societies. *Journal of Cross-Cultural Psychology* 34(3): 304–322.

[22]Oyserman, Daphna; Heather M. Coon, and Markus Kemmelmeier. 2002. Rethinking individualism and collectivism: Evaluation of theoretical assumptions and meta-analyses. *Psychological Bulletin* 128(1): 2–72.

[23]Lu, Lung-Tan. 2006. The Relationship between Cultural Distance and Performance in International Joint Ventures: A Critique and Ideas for Further Research. *International Journal of Management, 23* (3) p.437.

[24]Hofstede, Geert. 1983. The cultural relativity of organizational practices and theories. *Journal of International Business Studies* 14(2): 75–89.

[25]Ibid.

[26]Ibid.

[27]Hofstede, Geert. 1980. Culture's Consequences: International differences in work-related values. Beverly Hills: Sage.

[28]Griffith, David; Michael Hu and John Ryans, Jr, 2000. Process Standardization across intra- and inter-cultural relationships. Journal of International Business Studies, 31(2), 303-325.

[29]Kemmelmeier, Markus; Eugene Burnstein; Krum Krunov; Petia Genkova; Chie Kanagara; Mathew Hirshberg; Hans-Peter Erb; Grazyna Wieczorkowska, and Kimberly Noels. 2003. Individualism, collectivism, and authoritarianism in seven societies. *Journal of Cross-Cultural Psychology* 34(3): 304–322.

[30]Hofstede, Geert. 1985. The interaction between national and organizational value systems. *Journal of Management Studies* 22(4): 347–357.

[31] Javidan Mansour and Robert J. House, 2001. Cultural Acumen for the Global manager: Lessons from GLOBE project. *Organizational Dynamics, 29*(4), 289-305.

[32]Daft, Richard. 1995. *Understanding Management*. New York: The Dryden Press.

[33]Javidan, Mansour and Robert J. House, 2001. Cultural Acumen for the Global manager: Lessons from GLOBE project. *Organizational Dynamics, 29*(4), 289-305.

[34]Hofstede, Geert. 1980. Culture's Consequences: International differences in work-related values. Beverly Hills: Sage.

[35]Ibid.

[36]Hofstede, Geert. 1983. The cultural relativity of organizational practices and theories. *Journal of International Business Studies* 14(2): 75–89.

[37]Ibid.

[38]Ibid.

[39]Ibid.

[40]Ibid.

[41]Selmer, Jan. 1996. What Expatriate Mangers Know about Work Values of their subordinates: Swedish Executives in Thailand. Management International Review, 36,231-243.

[42]Hofstede, Geert. 1991. Cultures and organizations. NY: McGraw-Hill.

[43]Trompenaars, Fons and Charles Hampden-Turner, 1998. *Riding the Waves of Culture: Understanding Diversity in Global Business*.2nd Ed. London: McGraw-Hill.

CHAPTER 2

[1]Based on the cultural dimensions developed by Hofstede [1](1983, 78–85), Simcha Ronen and Oded Shenkar [2](1985, 444–445), and the works of Hofstede[3] (1985) on national and organizational system, clusters of countries of similar work values, geographic location, language and religion.

[2]Harrison, Graeme, Jill L. McKinnon, Sarala Panchapakesan, and Mitzi Leung. 1994. The influence of culture on organizational design and planning and control in Australia and the United States compared with Singapore and Hong Kong. *Journal of International Financial Management & Accounting* 5(3): 242–261.

[3]Ronen, Simcha and Oded Shenkar. 1985. Clustering countries on attitudinal dimensions: A review and synthesis. *Academy of Management Review* 10(3): 435–455.

[4] Garibaldi de Hilal, Adriana Victoria. 2006. Brazilian National Culture, Organizational Culture and Cultural Agreement. *International journal of Cross Cultural Management.* 6 (2), 139-167.

[5]A study by Hofstede had placed Brazil in the Latin European cluster but two others, Sinuta & Greenwood, and Ronen and Kraut had placed it as an independent.

[6]India has variously been placed in the Anglo cluster (Sirota & `Greenwood, 1971), the Latin American cluster (Haire, Ghiselli, & Porter, 1966) and the Far East Cluster (Hofstede, 1980).

[7]Studies have variously placed Israel in the Anglo cluster[13] (Ronen & Kraut, 1977) and the Germanic cluster [14](Hofstede, 1980).

[8]Hofstede, Geert. 1980. Culture's Consequences: International differences in work-related values. Beverly Hills: Sage.

[9]Simcha Ronen and Oded Shenkar. 1985. Clustering Countries on Attitudinal Dimensions: A Review and Synthesis. Academy of Management Review, 10(3), 435-454.

[10]Hofstede, Geert. 1983. The cultural relativity of organizational practices and theories. *Journal of International Business Studies* 14(2): 75–89.

[11]Hofstede, Geert. 1980. Culture's Consequences: International differences in work-related values. Beverly Hills: Sage.

CHAPTER 3

[1]Kreitner, Robert and Angelo Kinicki. 2004. *Organizational Behavior*. New York: The McGraw-Hill Companies.

[2] Denhardt, B. Robert and Janet V. Denhardt. 2002. The new public service: Serving rather than steering. *Public Administration Review* 60(6): 549–560.

[3]Goa, Ge and Stella Ting-Toomey. 1998. *Communicating*

Effectively with the Chinese. Thousand Oaks, CA: Sage.

[4]Bouncken, B. Ricarda. 2004. Cultural diversity in entrepreneurial teams: Findings of new ventures in Germany. *Creativity & Innovation Management* 3(4): 240–253.

[5]Ting-Toomey, Stella. 1999. *Communicating Across Cultures*. New York: Guilford Press.

[6]Kreitner, Robert and Angelo Kinicki. 2002. *Organizational Behavior*. 5th ed. Boston: Irwin/McGraw-Hill.
[7]Ibid.

[8]Ibid.

[9]Brett, Jeanne; Kristin Behfar, and Mary C. Kern. 2006. Managing multicultural teams. *Harvard Business Review* 84(11): 84–92.

[10]Laroche, Michel and Roy Toffoli. 2002. Cultural and language effects on Chinese bilinguals and Canadian responses to advertising. *International Journal of Advertising* 21(4): 505–524.

[11]Ibid.

[12]Bouncken, B. Ricarda. 2004. Cultural diversity in entrepreneurial teams: Findings of new ventures in Germany. *Creativity & Innovation Management* 3(4): 240–253.

[13]Laroche, Michel and Roy Toffoli. 2002. Cultural and language effects on Chinese bilinguals and Canadian responses to advertising. *International Journal of Advertising* 21(4): 505–524.

[14]Dou, Wei-lin and George W. Clark Jr. 1999. Appreciating the diversity in multicultural communication styles. *Business*

Forum 24(3, 4): 54–61.

[15]Ibid.

[16]Ibid.

[17]Bird, Allan and Joyce S. Osland. 2006. Making sense of
intercultural collaboration. *International Studies of
Management & Organization* 35(4): 115–132.

[18]Cuthbertson, Jennifer. 2003. Business across cultures. *Business
Book Review* 22: 19.

[19]Kreitner, Robert and Angelo Kinicki. 2004. *Organizational
Behavior*. New York: The McGraw-Hill Companies.
.

[20]McCain, Barbara. 1996. Multicultural team learning: An
approach towards communication. *Management Decision*
34(6): 65–68.

[21]Taylor, Shirley. 2006. Communicating across cultures. *British
Journal of Administrative Management* 53: 12–13.

CHAPTER 4

[1]Elashmari, Farid and Philip R. Harris. 1998. *Multicultural
Management 2000: Essential Cultural Insights for Global
Business Success*. Houston, Texas: Gulf Publishing
Company.

[2]Hodgetts, Richard M., Fred Luthans and Jonathan Doh. 2005.
*International Management: Culture, Strategy, and
Behavior*. New York: McGraw-Hill.

[3]Kreitner, Robert and Angelo Kinicki. 2004. *Organizational
Behavior*. New York: The McGraw-Hill Companies.

[4]Hodgetts, Richard M; Fred Luthans, and Jonathan Doh. (2005). International Management: Culture, Strategy, and Behavior. New York: McGraw-Hill.

CHAPTER 5

[1]Bird, Allan and Joyce S. Osland. 2006. Making sense of intercultural collaboration. *International Studies of Management & Organization* 35(4): 115–132.

[2]Ibid.

[3]Lu, Lung-Tan. 2006. The relationship between cultural distance and performance in international joint ventures: A critique and ideas for further research. *International Journal of Management* 23(3): 436–445.

CHAPTER 6

[1]Hofstede, Geert. 1983. The cultural relativity of organizational practices and theories. *Journal of International Business Studies* 14(2): 75–89.
[2]Ibid.

[3]Cameron, Kim and Robert E. Quinn. 1999. Diagnosing and Changing Organizational structure: Based on the Competing Values Framework. *Reading*. MA: Addison-Wesley.

[4]Oliver, C. 1997. Sustainable Competitive Advantage: Combining Institutional & Resource-based Views. *Strategic Management Journal*, 18(9), 697-713

[5]North, Douglas Cecil. 1981. *Structure and Change in Economic History*. New York: Norton.

[6] [1]Kreitner, Robert and Angelo Kinicki. 2002. *Organizational Behavior*. 5th ed. Boston: Irwin/McGraw-Hill.

[7]Garibaldi de Hilal, Adriana Victoria. 2006. Brazilian National Culture, Organizational Culture and Cultural Agreement. *International journal of Cross Cultural Management*. 6 (2), 139-167.

[8]Ibid.

[9]Ibid.

[10]Hofstede, Geert. 1983. The cultural relativity of organizational practices and theories. *Journal of International Business Studies* 14(2): 75–89.

[11]Hofstede, Geert. 1985. The interaction between national and organizational value systems. *Journal of Management Studies* 22(4): 347–357.

[12]Hofstede, Geert. 1983. The cultural relativity of organizational practices and theories. *Journal of International Business Studies* 14(2): 75–89.

[13]Ibid.

[14]Hofstede , Geert. 1985. The interaction between national and organizational value systems. *Journal of Management Studies* 22(4): 347–357.

[15]Ibid.

[16]Ibid.

[17]Ibid.

[18]Harrison, Graeme; Jill L. McKinnon; Sarala Panchapakesan, and Mitzi Leung. 1994. The influence of culture on organizational design and planning and control in Australia and the United States compared with Singapore and Hong Kong. *Journal of International Financial Management & Accounting* 5(3): 242–261.

[19]Stahl, Glen O. 1979. Managerial Effectiveness in Developing Countries. *International Review of Administrative Sciences*, *4* (1), pp.1-5.

[20]Hodgetts, Richard M., Fred Luthans and Jonathan Doh. (2005). *International Management: Culture, Strategy, and Behavior*. New York: McGraw-Hill.

[21]Gomez-Mejia, Luis and Balkin, David B. 2002. *Management*. New York: The McGraw-Hill Companies.

[22]Hodgetts, M. Richards; Fred Luthans and Jonathan Doh. 2005. *International Management: Culture, Strategy, and Behavior*. New York: McGraw-Hill.

[23]Gomez-Mejia, Luis and David B. Balkin. 2002. *Management*. New York: The McGraw-Hill Companies.

[24]Nambudiri, C.N. and Salyadain, M. S. 1978. Management Problems and Practices-India and Nigeria. *Columbia Journal of World Business, 143* (2), pp. 62-71.

[25]Gomez-Mejia, Luis and David B. Balkin. 2002. *Management*. New York: The McGraw-Hill Companies.

[26]Hodgetts, Richard M., Fred Luthans and Jonathan Doh. 2005. *International Management: Culture, Strategy, and Behavior*. New York: McGraw-Hill.

CHAPTER 7

[1]Harrison, Graeme; Jill L. McKinnon; Sarala Panchapakesan, and Mitzi Leung. 1994. The influence of culture on organizational design and planning and control in Australia and the United States compared with Singapore and Hong Kong. *Journal of International Financial Management & Accounting* 5(3): 242–261.

[2]Hofstede, Geert. 1983. The cultural Relativity of organizational Practices and Theories, *Journal of International business Studies, 14* (2) pp75-89.

[3]Matveev, V. Alexei and Paul E. Nelson. 2004. Cross Cultural Communication Competence and Multicultural Team Performance: Perceptions of American and Russian Managers. *International Journal of Cross Cultural Management, 4*(2): 253-270.

[4]Adler, Nancy J. 1997. *International Dimensions of Organizational Behavior.* 3rd ed. Cincinnati: South-Western College.

[5]Puffer, Sheila M. 1993. A Riddle Wrapped in an Enigma: Demystifying Russian Managerial Motivation. *European Management Journal,* 11, 473-480.

[6]Kreitner, Robert and Angelo Kinicki. 2002. *Organizational Behavior.* 5th ed. Boston: Irwin/McGraw-Hill.

[7]Anakwe, Uzoamaka P., Murugan Anandarajan, and Magid Igbaria. (2000). Management Practices across Cultures: Role of Support in Technology Usage. J*ournal of International Business.* 31(4) pp. 653-666.

[8]Nambudiri, C.N. and M. S. Salyadain. 1978. Management Problems and Practices-India and Nigeria. *Columbia Journal of World Business, 143* (2), pp. 62-71.

[9] Triandis, C. Harry. 2004. The Many Dimensions of Culture. *Academy of Management Executive.*18 (1) pp.88-93.

[10]O'Shaughnessy, J. Nicholas. 1985. Strategy and the US cultural Bias. *European Journal of Marketing, 19*(40): 23-32.

[11]Mcshane, L. Steven and Mary Ann Van Glinov. 2004.

Organizational Behavior: Emerging Realities for the Workplace. New York: The McGraw-Hill Companies.

[12]Ibid.

[13] Hofstede, Geert. 1980. *Culture's Consequences: International differences in work-related values*. Beverly Hills: Sage.

[14]Ibid.

[15]Mcshane, L. Steven and Mary Ann Van Glinov. 2004. *Organizational Behavior: Emerging Realities for the Workplace*. New York: The McGraw-Hill Companies.

[16]Hofstede, Geert. 1980. *Culture's Consequences: International differences in work related-values*. Beverly Hills: Sage.

[17]Limbs, C. Eric and Timothy l. Fort. 2000. Nigerian Business Practices and Their Interface with Virtue Ethics. *Journal of Business Ethics*. 26 (2), pp. 169-179.

[18]Kirkman, L. Bradley and Debra L. Shapiro. 2001. The Impact of Cultural Values on job satisfaction and Organizational Commitment in Self-managing work teams: The mediating role of employee resistance. Academy of Management Journal, 44, 57-569.

CHAPTER 8

[1]Gibson, Cristina and Mary E. Zellmer-Bruhn. 2001. Metaphors and Meaning: An Intercultural Analysis of the Concept of Teamwork. Administrative Science Quarterly, 46, 274-303.

[2]Ibid.

[3]Ibid.

[4]Matveev, V. Alexei and Paul E. Nelson. 2004. Cross Cultural Communication Competence and Multicultural Team Performance: Perceptions of American and Russian Managers. *International Journal of Cross Cultural Management, 4*(2): 253-270.

[5]Ibid.

[6]Rath, Devashis. 2002. New Holland Tractors (India). *Asian Case Research Journal*, 6(1), pp. 55-84.

[7]Matveev, V. Alexei and Paul E. Nelson. 2004. Cross Cultural Communication Competence and Multicultural Team Performance: Perceptions of American and   Russian Managers. *International Journal of Cross Cultural Management, 4*(2): 253-270.

[8]Ibid.

[9]Lawrence, Barbara S. 1997. Perspective: The Black Box of Organizational Demography. *Organizational science*, 8 (1-22).

[10] Tung, Rosalie L. 1993. Managing Cross-national and Intra-national Diversity. Human Resource Management, 32(4), 461-77.

[11]Griffith, Hu, and Ryans, Jr, 2000. Process Standardization across Intra- and Inter Cultural Relationships. *Journal of International Business Studies*, 31(2), 303.

[12] Matveev, V. Alexei and Paul E. Nelson. 2004. Cross Cultural Communication Competence and Multicultural Team Performance: Perceptions of American and Russian Managers. *International Journal of Cross Cultural Management, 4*(2): 253-270.

[13]Ibid.

[14]Gibson, Cristina and Mary E. Zellmer-Bruhn. 2001. Metaphors and Meaning: An Intercultural Analysis of the Concept of Teamwork. *Administrative Science Quarterly, 46*, 274-303.

[15]Ibid.

[17]Matveev, V. Alexei and Paul E. Nelson. 2004. Cross Cultural Communication Competence and Multicultural Team Performance: Perceptions of American and Russian Managers. International Journal of Cross Cultural Management, 4(2): 253-270.

[18]Ibid.

[19]Gibson, Cristina and Mary E. Zellmer-Bruhn. 2001. Metaphors and Meaning: An Intercultural Analysis of the Concept of Teamwork. Administrative Science Quarterly, 46, 274-303.

[20]Ibid.

[21]Bantz, Charles R. 1993. Cultural Diversity and Group Cross-cultural Team Research. *Journal of applied Communication Research, 1(20).*

[22]Matveev, V. Alexei and Paul E. Nelson. 2004. Cross Cultural Communication Competence and Multicultural Team Performance: Perceptions of American and Russian Managers. *International Journal of Cross Cultural Management, 4(2): 253-270.*

[23]Mcshane, L. Steven and Mary Ann Van Glinov. 2004. *Organizational Behavior: Emerging Realities for the Workplace.* New York: The McGraw-Hill Companies.

[24] Matveev, V. Alexei and Paul E. Nelson. 2004. Cross Cultural

Communication Competence and Multicultural Team Performance: Perceptions of American and Russian Managers. *International Journal of Cross Cultural Management, 4*(2): 253-270.

[25]Bantz, Charles R. 1993. Cultural Diversity and Group Cross-cultural Team Research. *Journal of applied Communication Research, 1*(20).

[26]Matveev, V. Alexei and Paul E. Nelson. 2004. Cross Cultural Communication Competence and Multicultural Team Performance: Perceptions of American and Russian Managers. *International Journal of Cross Cultural Management*, 4(2): 253-270.

[27]Kreitner, Robert and Angelo Kinicki. 2002. *Organizational Behavior*. 5th ed. Boston: Irwin/McGraw-Hill.

[28]Matveev, V. Alexei and Paul E. Nelson. 2004. Cross Cultural Communication Competence and Multicultural Team Performance: Perceptions of American and Russian Managers. *International Journal of Cross Cultural Management, 4*(2): 253-270.

[29]Hodgetts, M. Richard; Fred Luthans and Jonathan Doh. 2005. *International Management: Culture, Strategy, and Behavior*. New York: McGraw-Hill.

[30]Matveev, V. Alexei and Paul E. Nelson. 2004. Cross Cultural Communication Competence and Multicultural Team Performance: Perceptions of American and Russian Managers. *International Journal of Cross Cultural Management, 4*(2): 253-270.

[31]Ibid.

[32]Ibid.

[33]Goa, Ge, and Stella Ting-Toomey. 1998. *Communicating Effectively with the Chinese*. Thousand Oaks, CA: Sage.

[34]Dou, Wei-lin and George W. Clark Jr. 1999. Appreciating the diversity in multicultural communication styles. *Business Forum* 24(3, 4): 54–61.

[35]Matveev, V. Alexei and Paul E. Nelson. 2004. Cross Cultural Communication Competence and Multicultural Team Performance: Perceptions of American and Russian Managers. *International Journal of Cross Cultural Management, 4*(2): 253-270.

[36]Ibid.

[37]Gudykunst, William B. 1998. Applying Anxiety/Uncertainty Management (AUM) Theory to Intercultural Adjustment Training. *International Journal of Intercultural Relations* 22: 227-50.

[38]Tuleja, Elizabeth and James S. O'Rourke, IV. 2008. Intercultural communication for business. Mason, OH: South Western Cangage Learning.

[39] Grosse, Christine Uber. 2002. Managing communication within virtual intercultural teams. *Business Communication Quarterly* 65(4): 22–38.

[40]Milliman, John; Sully Taylor and Andrew J. Czaplewski. 2000. Cross-Cultural Performance Feedback in Multinational Enterprises: Opportunity for organizational Learning. *Human Resources Planning, 25*(3), p. 29.

[41]Ibid

[42]Dou, Wei-lin, and George W. Clark Jr. 1999. Appreciating the

diversity in multicultural communication styles. *Business Forum* 24(3, 4): 54–61.

[43]Stoner, James; Arthur Finch, and R. Edward Freeman. 1989. *Management*. 4th ed. Upper Saddle River. New Jersey: Prentice-Hall.

[44] Grosse, Christine Uber. 2002. Managing communication within virtual intercultural teams. *Business Communication Quarterly* 65(4): 22–38.

[45]Kreitner, Robert and Angelo Kinicki. 2002. *Organizational Behavior*. 5th ed. Boston: Irwin/McGraw-Hill.

[46]Mcshane, L. Steven and Mary Ann Van Glinov. 2004. *Organizational Behavior: Emerging Realities for the Workplace*. New York: The McGraw-Hill Companies.

[47]Grosse, Christine Uber. 2002. Managing communication within virtual intercultural teams. *Business Communication Quarterly* 65(4): 22–38.

[48]Ibid.

CHAPTER 9

[1]Singh, Niti and Venkat Krishnan. 2007. Transformational Leadership in India: Developing and validating a new scale using the grounded theory approach. *International journal of Cross Cultural Management, 7(2), 219-236.*

[2]House, Robert J., Paul J. Hanges, Mansour Javidan, Peter Dorfman, and Vipin Gupta. 2004. *Culture, Leadership, and Organizations. The GLOBE Study of 62 Societies.* Sage, CA: Thousand Oaks.

[3]Yeganeh, Hamid and Zhan Su. 2006. Conceptual Foundations of Cultural Management Research, *International journal of*

Cross Cultural Management, 6(3), 361-76.

[4]Singh, Niti and Venkat Krishnan. 2007. Transformational Leadership in India: Developing and validating a new scale using the grounded theory approach. *International journal of Cross Cultural Management,7(2), 219-236.*

[5]Van de Vliert, Evert. 2006. Autocratic Leadership around the Globe: Do climate and wealth drive leadership culture? *Journal of Cross Cultural psychology, 37(1), 42-59.*

[6]Van Emmerik, Hetty; Martin C. Euwema, and Hein Wendt. 2008. Leadership Behaviors around the World: The relative importance of gender versus cultural background. *International journal of Cross Cultural Management*, 8 (3), 297-315.

[7]House, Robert J., Paul J. Hanges, Mansour Javidan, Peter Dorfman, and Vipin Gupta. 2004. *Culture, Leadership, and Organizations. The GLOBE Study of 62 Societies.* Sage, CA: Thousand Oaks.

[8]Chhokar, Jagdeep; Felix C. Brodbeck and Robert J. House. 2007. *Culture and leadership across the World: The GLOBE Book of In-depth studies of 25 societies.* New York: Taylor and Francis Group.

[9]Van Emmerik, Hetty; Martin C. Euwema, and Hein Wendt. 2008. Leadership Behaviors around the World: The relative importance of gender versus cultural background. *International journal of Cross Cultural Management*, 8 (3), 297-315.

[10]Van de Vliert, Evert. 2006. Autocratic Leadership around the Globe: Do climate and wealth drive leadership culture? *Journal of Cross Cultural psychology, 37(1), 42-59.*

[11]Chhokar, Jagdeep; Felix C. Brodbeck and Robert J. House. 2007. *Culture and leadership across the World: The GLOBE Book of In-depth studies of 25 societies.* New York: Taylor and Francis Group.

[12]Van Emmerik, Hetty; Martin C. Euwema, and Hein Wendt. 2008. Leadership Behaviors around the World: The relative importance of gender versus cultural background. *International journal of Cross Cultural Management,* 8 (3), 297-315.

[13]Casimir, Gian and David A. Waldman. 2007. A cross cultural comparison of the importance of leadership traits for effective low-level and high-level leaders: Australia and China. *International journal of Cross Cultural Management, 7(1), 47-80.*

[14]House, Robert J., Paul J. Hanges, Mansour Javidan, Peter Dorfman, and Vipin Gupta. 2004. *Culture, Leadership, and Organizations. The GLOBE Study of 62 Societies.* Sage, CA: Thousand Oaks.

[15]Ibid.

[16]Van Emmerik, Hetty; Martin C. Euwema, and Hein Wendt. 2008. Leadership Behaviors around the World: The relative importance of gender versus cultural background. *International journal of Cross Cultural Management,* 8 (3), 297-315.

[17] Singh, Niti and Venkat Krishnan. 2007. Transformational Leadership in India: Developing and validating a new scale using the grounded theory approach. *International journal of Cross Cultural Management, 7(2), 219-236.*

[18]Hosfsede, Geert. 1983. The cultural Relativity of organizational Practices and Theories, *Journal of International business*

Studies, 14 (2) pp75-89.

[19]Ibid.

[20]Ibid.

[21]Ibid.

[22]Ibid.

[23]Ibid.

[24]Ibid.

[25]Ibid.

[26]Ibid.

[27]Hofstede, Geert. 1985. The interaction between national and organizational value systems. *Journal of Management Studies* 22(4): 347–357.

[28]Harrison, Graeme; Jill L. McKinnon, Sarala Panchapakesan, and Mitzi Leung. 1994. The influence of culture on organizational design and planning and control in Australia and the United States compared with Singapore and Hong Kong. *Journal of International Financial Management & Accounting* 5(3): 242–261.

[29]Van de Vliert, Evert. 2006. Autocratic Leadership around the Globe: Do climate and wealth drive leadership culture? *Journal of Cross Cultural psychology, 37(1), 42-59.*

[30]Mendonca, Manuel and Rabindra N. Kanungo. 1996. Impact of culture on Performance Management in Developing Countries. *International Journal of Manpower*, 17(4-5), pp.65-76.

[31]Mcshane, L. Steven and Mary Ann Van Glinov. 2004. *Organizational Behavior: Emerging Realities for the Workplace.* New York: The McGraw-Hill Companies.

[32]Ibid.

[33]Kreitner, Robert and Angelo Kinicki. 2002. *Organizational Behavior.* 5th ed. Boston: Irwin/McGraw-Hill.
[34]Ibid.

[35]Ibid.

CHAPTER 10

[1]Beamer, Linda and Iris Varner, 2001. *Intercultural communication in Global workplace.* New York: The McGraw-Hill Companies.

[2] Metcalf, Lynn E., Allan Bird; Mark F. Peterson; Mahesh Shankarmahesh; and Terri R. Lituchy. 2007. Cultural Influences in Negotiations: A four country comparative analysis. *International journal of Cross Cultural Management,* 7 (2), 147-168.

[3]Hofstede, Geert. 2001. *Cultures Consequences: Comparing values, Behaviors, Institutions, organizations across Nations.* 2nd Ed. Sage, CA: Thousand Oaks.

[4]Metcalf, Lynn E., Allan Bird; Mark F. Peterson; Mahesh Shankarmahesh; and Terri R. Lituchy. 2007. Cultural Influences in Negotiations: A four country comparative analysis. *International journal of Cross Cultural Management,* 7 (2), 147-168.

[5]Hofstede, Geert. 2001. *Cultures Consequences: Comparing values, Behaviors, Institutions, organizations Across Nations.* 2nd Ed. Sage, CA: Thousand Oaks.

[6]Ibid.

[7]Ibid.

[8]Metcalf, Lynn E., Allan Bird; Mark F. Peterson; Mahesh Shankarmahesh; and Terri R. Lituchy. 2007. Cultural Influences in Negotiations: A four country comparative analysis. *International journal of Cross Cultural Management,* 7 (2), 147-168.

[9]Lewicki, Roy J; Bruce Barry, and David M. Saunders. 2009. *Negotiations: Readings, Exercises and Cases.* 6th Ed. New York: McGraw-Hill.

[10]Ibid.

[11] Metcalf, Lynn E., Allan Bird; Mark F. Peterson; Mahesh Shankarmahesh; and Terri R. Lituchy. 2007. Cultural Influences in Negotiations: A four country comparative analysis. *International journal of Cross Cultural Management,* 7 (2), 147-168.

[12]Lewicki, Roy J., Bruce Barry, and David M. Saunders. 2009. *Negotiations: Readings, Exercises and Cases.* 6th Ed. New York: McGraw-Hill.

[13]Ibid.

[14]Ibid.

[15]Ibid.

[16]Metcalf, Lynn E; Allan Bird, Mark F. Peterson, Mahesh Shankarmahesh; and Terri R. Lituchy. 2007. Cultural Influences in Negotiations: A four country comparative analysis. *International journal of Cross Cultural*

Management, 7 (2), 147-168.

CHAPTER 11

[1]Pfeffer, Jeffrey and Philips Nowak. 1976. Joint Ventures and Interorganizational Interdependence. *Administrative Science Quarterly*, 21, 398-418.

[2]Kreitner, Robert and Angelo Kinicki. 2002. *Organizational Behavior.* 5th ed. Boston: Irwin/McGraw-Hill.
[3]Ibid.

[4]Selmer, Jan and Corinna T. de Leon. 2002. Parent cultural control of Foreign subsidiaries through organizational acculturation: a longitudinal study. *Int. J. of Human Resource Management,* p. 1150.

[5]Dou, Wei-lin and George W. Clark Jr. 1999. Appreciating the diversity in multicultural communication styles. *Business Forum* 24(3, 4): 54–61.

[6]Tuleja, Elizabeth and James S. O'Rourke, IV. 2008. *Intercultural communication for business.* Mason, OH: South Western Cangage Learning.

[7]Dou, Wei-lin and George W. Clark Jr. 1999. Appreciating the diversity in multicultural communication styles. *Business Forum* 24(3, 4): 54–61.

[8] Hodgetts, Richard M., Fred Luthans and Jonathan Doh. 2005. *International Management: Culture, Strategy, and Behavior.* New York: McGraw-Hill.

[9]Hofstede, Geert. 1983. The cultural Relativity of organizational Practices and Theories, *Journal of International business Studies,* Volume *14* (2) pp75-89.

[10] Oliver, C. 1997. Sustainable Competitive Advantage: Combining Institutional and Resource-Based Views. *Strategic Management Journal, 18*, 697-713.

[11] Kreitner, Robert and Angelo Kinicki. 2002. *Organizational Behavior*. 5th ed. Boston: Irwin/McGraw-Hill.

[12] Kogut Bruce. 1991. Country Capabilities and the permeability of Borders. *Strategic Management Journal*. Vol. 12, pp. 33-48.

[13] Cuthbertson, Jennifer. 2003. Business across cultures. *Business Book Review* 22: 19.

[14] Kogut, Bruce and Harbir Singh. 1988. The Effect of National Culture on the Choice of Entry Mode. *Journal of Business Studies,19* (3), pp. 411-432.

[15] Chen, Min. 1995. *Asian Management Systems: Chinese, Japanese, and Korean Styles of Business*. New York: Routledge.

[16] Jang, S and Chang, M.H.1995. Discursive Contradiction Between Traditional and Modernity in Korean Management Practices. *'A case of Samsung's New Management"*, paper presented at 12th EGOS Colloquium, Istanbul, Turkey.

[17] Li, Ji, Kevin Lam and Gongming Qian. 2001. Does Culture Affect Behavior and Performance of Firms? The Case of Joint Ventures in China. *Journal of International Business Studies,* 32(1), 115.

[18] Cuthbertson, Jennifer. 2003. Business across cultures. *Business Book Review* 22: 19.

[19] Ibid.

[20]Ibid.

[21]Dou, Wei-lin and George W. Clark Jr. 1999. Appreciating the diversity in multicultural communication styles. *Business Forum* 24(3, 4): 54–61.

[22]Evans, Paul; Vladimir Pucik, and Jean-Louis Barsoux. 2002. *The Global Challenge: Frameworks for International Human Resource Management.* New York: The McGraw-Hill Companies.

[23]Kreitner, Robert and Angelo Kinicki. 2002. *Organizational Behavior.* 5th ed. Boston: Irwin/McGraw-Hill.

[24]Evans, Paul; Vladimir Pucik, and Jean-Louis Barsoux. 2002. *The Global Challenge: Frameworks for International Human Resource Management.* New York: The McGraw-Hill Companies.

[25]Cuthbertson, Jennifer. 2003. Business across cultures. *Business Book Review* 22: 19.

[26]Ibid.

[27]Evans, Paul; Vladimir Pucik, and Jean-Louis Barsoux. 2002. *The Global Challenge: Frameworks for International Human Resource Management.* New York: The McGraw-Hill Companies.

[28]Grosse, Christine Uber. 2002. Managing communication within virtual intercultural teams. *Business Communication Quarterly* 65(4): 22–38.

[29]Tuleja, Elizabeth and James S. O'Rourke, IV. 2008. *Intercultural communication for business.* Mason, OH: South Western Cangage Learning.

[30]McCain, Barbara. 1996. Multicultural team learning: An approach towards communication. *Management Decision* 34(6): 65–68.

CHAPTER 12

[1]Hodgetts, Richard M., Fred Luthans and Jonathan Doh. 2005. *International Management: Culture, Strategy, and Behavior.* New York: McGraw-Hill.

[2]Ibid.

[3]Brett, Jeanne, Kristin Behfar, and Mary C. Kern. 2006. Managing multicultural teams. *Harvard Business Review* 84(11): 84–92.

[4]Tokarek, Margaret. 2006. How to manage intercultural communication. *People Management* 12(21): 66–67.

[5]Dou, Wei-lin, and George W. Clark Jr. 1999. Appreciating the diversity in multicultural communication styles. *Business Forum* 24(3, 4): 54–61.

[7]Taylor, Shirley. 2006. Communicating across cultures. *British Journal of Administrative Management* 53: 12–13.

[8]Tokarek, Margaret. 2006. How to manage intercultural communication. *People Management* 12(21): 66–67.

[9]Dou, Wei-lin, and George W. Clark Jr. 1999. Appreciating the diversity in multicultural communication styles. *Business Forum* 24(3, 4): 54–61.

[10]Taylor, Shirley. 2006. Communicating across cultures. *British Journal of Administrative Management* 53: 12–13.

[11]Asad, Talal. 2003. Boundaries and Rights in Islamic Law:

Introduction. *Social Research*, 70(3), pp. 683-686.

[12]Frausto, Carol. 2000. A woman's perspective to doing business in the Kingdom of Saudi Arabia. *Westchester County Business Journal* 39(8): 22.

[13]Tokarek, Margaret. 2006. How to manage intercultural communication. *People Management* 12(21): 66–67.

[14]Hodgetts, Richard M., Fred Luthans and Jonathan Doh. 2005. *International Management: Culture, Strategy, and Behavior.* New York: McGraw-Hill.

[15]Lewicki, Roy J; Bruce Barry, and David M. Saunders. 2009. *Negotiations: Readings, Exercises and Cases.* 6th Ed. New York: McGraw-Hill.

[16] Hodgetts, Richard M., Fred Luthans and Jonathan Doh. 2005. *International Management: Culture, Strategy, and Behavior.* New York: McGraw-Hill.

[17]Tokarek, Margaret. 2006. How to manage intercultural communication. *People Management* 12(21): 66–67.

[18]Ibid.

[19]Billikopf-Encina, Gregorio. 2000. Communicating across cultures (book). *International Journal of Conflict Management* 11(4): 378–388.

[20]Lewicki, Roy J., Bruce Barry and David M. Saunders. 2009. *Negotiations: Readings, Exercises and Cases.* 6th Ed. New York: McGraw-Hill.

[21]Hanson, Jennifer and Wanda Fox. 1995. Communicating across cultures. *Training & Development* 49(1): 56–59.

[22]Grosse, Christine Uber. 2002. Managing communication within virtual intercultural teams. *Business Communication Quarterly* 65(4): 22–38.

[23]Ibid.
[24]Ibid.

[25]Hodgetts, Richard M., Fred Luthans and Jonathan Doh. 2005. *International Management: Culture, Strategy, and Behavior.* New York: McGraw-Hill.

[26]Hanson, Jennifer and Wanda Fox. 1995. Communicating across cultures. *Training & Development* 49(1): 56–59.

[27]Ting-Toomey, Stella. 1999. *Communicating Across Cultures.* New York: Guilford Press.

[28]Hanson, Jennifer and Wanda Fox. 1995. Communicating across cultures. *Training & Development* 49(1): 56–59.

[29]Dou, Wei-lin and George W. Clark Jr. 1999. Appreciating the diversity in multicultural communication styles. *Business Forum* 24(3, 4): 54–61.

[30]Kreitner, Robert and Angelo Kinicki. 2004. *Organizational Behavior.* New York: The McGraw-Hill Companies.

CHAPTER 13

[1]Hodgetts, Richard M., Fred Luthans, and Jonathan Doh. 2005. *International Management: Culture, Strategy, and Behavior.* New York: McGraw-Hill.

[2]Burack, Elmer H., Marvin D. Burack; Diane M. Miller, and Kathleen Morgan. 1994. New Paradigm Approaches in Strategic Human Resource Management. *Group and Organization Management.* 19 (1), 141-159.

[3]Culpan, Oya and Gillian H. Wright. 2002. Women abroad:
Getting the best results from women managers.
International Journal of Human Resources 13(5): 784–801.

[4]Hodgetts, Richard M., Fred Luthans and Jonathan Doh. 2005.
*International Management: Culture, Strategy, and
Behavior.* New York: McGraw-Hill.

[5]Ibid.

[6]Culpan, Oya and Gillian H. Wright. 2002. Women abroad:
Getting the best results from women managers.
International Journal of Human Resources 13(5): 784–801.

[7]Dou, Wei-lin and George W. Clark Jr. 1999. Appreciating the
diversity in multicultural communication styles. *Business
Forum* 24(3, 4): 54–61.

[8]Hodgetts, Richard M., Fred Luthans and Jonathan Doh. 2005.
*International Management: Culture, Strategy, and
Behavior.* New York: McGraw-Hill.

[9]Takeuchi, Riki; Seokhwa Yun, and Joyce E. Russell. 2002.
Antecedents and Consequences of the Perceived
Adjustment of Japanese Expatriates in the USA.
International Journal of Human Resource, 13(8)1224-
1244.

[10]Hodgetts, Richard M., Fred Luthans and Jonathan Doh. 2005.
*International Management: Culture, Strategy, and
Behavior.* New York: McGraw-Hill.

[11]Adler, Nancy J. 1997. *International Dimensions of
Organizational Behavior.* 3rd Ed. Cincinnati: South-
Western College.

[12]McCain, Barbara. 1996. Multicultural team learning: An approach towards communication. *Management Decision* 34(6): 65–68.

[13]Dou, Wei-lin and George W. Clark Jr. 1999. Appreciating the diversity in multicultural communication styles. *Business Forum* 24(3, 4): 54–61.

[14]McCain, Barbara. 1996. Multicultural team learning: An approach towards communication. *Management Decision* 34(6): 65–68.

[15]Matveev, Alexei, Nagesh Rao and Richard Milter. 2001. *Developing a Scale to Measure Intercultural Communication Competence: A pilot Study in Multicultural Organization.* Paper submitted to the International and Intercultural communications Division of the National Communication Association, Atlanta, November, 2001.

[16]Matveev, V. Alexei and Paul E. Nelson. 2004. Cross Cultural Communication Competence and Multicultural Team Performance: Perceptions of American and Russian Managers. *International Journal of Cross Cultural Management,* 4(2): 253-270.

[17]Ibid.
[18]Ibid.

CHAPTER 14

[1]Moran, Robert; Philip Harris, and Sarah Moran. 2007. *Managing Cultural Difference: Global Leadership Strategies for the 21ˢᵗ Century.* Burlington, MA: Butterworth Heinemann

[2]Ibid.

[3]Takeuchi, Riki; Seokhwa Yun and Joyce E. Russell. 2002.

Antecedents and Consequences of the Perceived
Adjustment of Japanese Expatriates in the USA.
International Journal of Human Resource, 13(8)1224-
1244.

[4]Daft, L. Richard. 1995. *Understanding Management*. New York:
The Dryden Press.
[5]Ibid

[6]Takeuchi, Riki; Seokhwa Yun, and Joyce E. Russell. 2002.
Antecedents and Consequences of the Perceived
Adjustment of Japanese Expatriates in the USA.
International Journal of Human Resource, *13*(8)1224-
1244.

CHAPTER 15

[1]Stoner, James; Arthur Finch, and Edward R. Freeman. 1989.
Management. 4th ed. Upper Saddle River. New Jersey:
Prentice-Hall.
[2]Ibid.

.[3]Swaidan, Ziad; Scott J. Vitell, and Mohammed Y.A. Rawwas.
2003. Consumer ethics: Determinants of ethical beliefs
African Americans. *Journal of Business Ethics* 46(2): 175–
186.

[4]Johnson, E. Craig. 2007. *Meeting the Ethical Challenges of
Leadership: Casting Light or Shadow*. Thousand Oaks,
CA: Sage.

[5]Lan, Zhiyong and Kathleen K. Anders. 2000. A paradigmatic
view of contemporary public administration research: An
empirical test. *Administration & Society* 32(2): 138–165.

[6]Dowling, J. Peter; Denice E. Welch, and Randall S. Schuler.
1999. *International human resource management.*
Cincinnati: South-Western College Publishing.

www.ingramcontent.com/pod-product-compliance
Lightning Source LLC
Chambersburg PA
CBHW032303210326
41520CB00047B/1040